FLOWERS for MARÍA SUCEL

FLOWERS for MARÍA SUCEL

William Castaño-Bedoya

A Novel

BOOK&BILIAS
Coral Gables

Copyright © 2022 William Castaño-Bedoya

All rights are reserved. No part of this publication may be reproduced, distributed, or transmitted in any form or by any means. Inlcuding photocopying, recording, or other electronic or mechanical methods, without the prior written permission of the publisher, except in the case of brief quotations embodied in critical reviews and certain other noncommercial uses permitted by copyright law. For permission requests, write to the publisher, addressed "Attention: permissions coordinator," at the address below, or email to literaryworld@bookandbilias.us

ISBN 978-1-7369168-8-9 (Paperback English edition)
ISBN 978-1-7369168-9-6 (Hardcover English edition)
ISBN 978-0-9788452-4-7 (e-Book English edition)
ISBN 978-1-7369168-0-3 (Paperback Spanish edition)
ISBN 978-1-7369168-1-0 (Hardcover Spanish edition)
ISBN 978-1-7369168-2-7 (e-Book Spanish edition)
ISBN 978-1-7369168-3-4 (Audiobook Spanish edition)

Library of Congress Control Number: 0000000000

Any references to historical events, real people, or real places are used fictitiously. Names, characters, and places are products of the author's imagination.

Front Cover image and Book Design by: William Castaño-Bedoya.

Printed By Ingram, in the United States of America.

First printing edition in English language 2022.

Book&Bilias
Coral Gables, FL 33146
www.bookandbilias.us

*Work edited with the support of the Reading
Colombia Program Co-financing for
translation*

*For Gilberto and María Sucel, for all eternity.
For Dora-Luz, and for my children Willie and Camila,
with all my heart.
For my brothers and sisters, orphaned as well.*

Who am I to judge the old folks?

Contents

Gilberto	15
Asphalt Coffee	25
In Times of Hitler and Other Things	45
Mediums and Spirits	55
They Wouldn't Serve Them…	69
Between Bogotá and the Plains	85
The Acrostic	95
Flowers	113
Juan de Dios	127
Page Nine Hundred Seventy…	147
An Old Rattletrap Bus	161
In Paradise	171
Ofir… Ofir…	185
Something Other Than a Prayer	197
When Picasso Died	213
Farewell to the Older Ones	225
Still Waters	239
The Door Opened	259

Gilberto

... 1938

Gilberto, as Doña Sara had christened him, was about twenty when she gave him the worst thrashing of his life. Nobody knew about it because it hapapened behind closed doors, but it was seared into his memory—not only because he almost fainted from the pain to the scruff of his neck, but because she threw him out after she was done. His mother felt justified in doing so because he had spent a month's worth of market money to rent an American car that some fair-weather scoundrel had brought to the town as a novelty, as nobody there had ever seen an automobile.

He thus became a sort of exile wandering through the villages and hamlets of Viejo Caldas plying any type of street trade he could find. Gilberto most liked to hang around in bars, to be near the women who frequented them, and the night hours were his preferred time for finding odd jobs; he would guide the drunks unable to find their way home and charge them for his services. He slept in fleabag hotels near the brothels where the whores took their clients; there, whether he wanted to or not, the sounds and images filtering through the cracks in the walls made him a silent witness to the sexual encounters of the sleepless unfaithful. Little did he care about the infidelities next door. The only important thing for him was to rest. At noon, he had to go out for his first coffee and improvise the day again. Part of his morning ritual, was to visit the town's church to deposit some coins in the alms box and light two candles. Despite the dissipated life he circumstantially lived, he was a character who did not owe anything to anyone but to his own conscience; he did not know how many children he had or where they were.

One very early morning during his exile, as he roamed the streets of a small town called Salamina, where he had arrived a few months earlier, Gilberto decided to go inside the Church of the Immaculate Conception. He noticed that the benches were beginning to fill with parishioners, who were quietly chatting, cheerfully and familiarly. He supposed that there would soon be a special ceremony, because carefully dressed people continued to arrive.

In those days he didn't much care for going to mass, though he would sometimes pass through a church and lay a few coins in the collection tray for the candles, lighting some, making the sign of the cross before leaving. But he was distracted that morning, watching the women who went inside in groups, dressed in dark, discreetly elegant clothing, their heads covered with lacy black shawls. The men accompanying them were also dressed in black or dark gray, their white shirts with small, starched collars surrounding limp, dark ties. Most of them held felt hats in their hands, having taken them off when entering the church.

When the church was almost full, a lovely, straight-haired woman walked in, holding a peacefully sleeping baby in her arms. She was with a man who appeared to be her husband, and as they approached the altar together, they quietly greeted their acquaintances with timid, blushing nods. Gilberto observed them carefully and couldn't help feeling a healthy dose of envy. He leaned against one of the columns that flanked the length of the church and watched the events as they unfolded.

Suddenly, the baby cried, almost imperceptibly. The lady rocked it immediately, sweetly hushing it until the baby was quiet, though still awake.

Altar boys entered from the vestry, and women who took care of preparing things for the service, and they went to greet the woman with the child in her arms. After admiring the baby's cooing face, they smiled and chatted pleasantly, then walked away. The baby unexpectedly spit its pacifier out onto the floor, undetected by its mother. With his characteristic gentlemanliness, Gilberto picked it up and handed it to the lady. He was aware that his good looks made the girls blush, and although this time that wasn't his intention, when she met his eyes upon receiving the pacifier the woman was unsettled. The baby's father arrived solicitously to assist his wife and politely thanked Gilberto.

"What a cute little boy," said Gilberto.

"She's a girl, and today is her baptism," the man explained.

Gilberto apologized for mistaking the child's gender and excused himself, embarrassed. He slipped away to sit on one of the benches. The child had apparently touched him; maybe he envisioned the face of a daughter he might never have known, and he decided to stay for the ceremony. When the priest mentioned the baptismal details, he took a pen from his shirt pocket and jotted them down as the priest poured holy water and prayed: "I baptize thee María Sucel Baroja Sánchez, in the name of the Father, the Son, and the Holy Spirit, to bring light and joy to the home of Don Elías Baroja and Doña Isabelina Sánchez."

Gilberto recalled his parents and for a moment imagined himself as a child. He did not leave the church until the ceremony was about to end; he gave some beggars a few coins and stood on the steps to the atrium while he lit up a cigarette, finally blending into the people exiting the church. The young woman holding the baby girl saw him and thought to speak to him. He was politely acknowledging people who nodded to him as Isabelina approached and thanked him for his trouble.

"It was nothing, ma'am! God bless your daughter," he replied in a deep, commanding voice. Isabelina was pleasantly impressed, though she didn't quite understand why she felt such an affinity with this man, in whose eyes she recognized a depth of feeling. Intrigued, the young man's eyes followed her as she walked away, turning to look back at him occasionally.

He finally put out his cigarette and walked away along the sidewalk towards some shops where guitars and violins could be heard playing milongas. But his attention was drawn to a bar where a group of men chatted on wooden stools. He recognized a cheerful Elías among them. Sensing that his fate was somehow linked to the couple from the church, he decided to sit near the men, at a table for two. Elías saw him and waved him over. Gilberto was grateful for such a day, so different from every other day during the months of his exile, and for having been welcomed so warmly by people who didn't even know him. He dragged his chair over to Elías's table and thanked the men for their welcome as he made eye contact with each directly.

"Thank you, sir! My name is Gilberto Cervantes, and I am from Neira." Elías pushed his chair back and stood politely, smiling broadly and generously.

"Pleased to meet you, young man, I am Elías Baroja and am truly happy to make your acquaintance. Welcome to our table!" There was a flurry of hand-shaking and introductions, which included the man's father and father-in-law. They chatted for only twenty minutes, because Elías was merely entertaining a few close relatives while Isabelina and some neighbor ladies prepared lunch for the guests. Then, realizing he was an outsider, Gilberto bid them farewell and thanked them. Elías suggested that he go to the work camp to see what type of work was available. Gilberto had learned during the conversation that the baptized baby's father was the respected supervisor of a crew of over one hundred men charged with painstakingly digging the roads across which coffee from the Viejo Caldas plantations would reach the world.

Walking farther along that same street, Gilberto arrived at a bar where he usually had his breakfast coffee and greeted Nélida, the waitress he had befriended a few weeks earlier. When she saw him, she discreetly indicated two men chatting and getting drunk on , whispering to him that they were from the military and might be recruiting young men for the army.

Gilberto paled and bit his lip. This bit of news clashed with the joy he had just been feeling. What will be, will be, and if my fate lies with the army, then so be it and I won't hide. God will decide! he thought decisively as he approached the bar, taking a seat and asking Nélida to bring him something strong to drink. She first poured him a glass of water, and then brought a double shot of , some lemon wedges and a salt shaker. Gilberto took a lemon wedge, sprinkled it with salt, and drank the spirits in a single swallow, chasing it down with a generous sip of water. He then squeezed the salty lemon wedge into his mouth, and, turning slightly to his left, took a wrinkled white handkerchief from his back pocket and wiped his mouth and mustache several times. He winked at the waitress, who was worriedly gesturing at him to leave.

The minutes passed, and already he had consumed half a bottle of and his forehead was bathed in sweat. He drank, he spit, and he smoked. The sources of his fear were also drinking while putting coins into the slot of a jukebox to make it play music.

As he neared the table where the men sat, Gilberto asked somewhat flippantly, "Do you think I'm suitable to join the military?" The men looked at each other, realized the anise-flavored liqueur was making him brave, and just continued their conversation, ignoring him.

"Can you tell me if I'm eligible for the army? What's the secret to getting accepted all the way?" he insisted.

"Why so eager?" one of them answered, disdainfully.

"I have nowhere to sleep tonight or tomorrow, and though I'm not hungry, I have nowhere to eat," he boldly declared.

"Don't you think that in the army there's nowhere to sleep either, and not much to eat?" asked the officer, annoyed, as he looked away.

The other soldier laughed once, loudly, merely encouraging the young man's boldness. Defiant, Gilberto replied, "I don't care!"

"Sit down, boy," confided one of them as he took

Gilberto's arm. "We're not recruiting! It's our day off, and we're enjoying some . Why don't you join us and tell us about this town? Don't ruin this nice day for us."

Gilberto sat down and secretly turned to look at Nélida, letting her know with a slight lift of his eyebrow and a wicked gaze that there was nothing wrong. "If you are new to this wonderful Caldas, then where are you from?" he asked.

One of them shook his pack of unfiltered cigarettes, pulled one out and tapped the tip repeatedly against his left thumbnail, saying that they were from somewhere near Bogotá and were in the area on a recruiting mission.

"I see why you are unfamiliar with Caldas. You're not from around here. So ... what do you think?" asked Gilberto.

Shrugging, the quieter one suggested that it was fine and told him that he preferred the women from this coffee-growing area because they were beautiful.

"Do you want me to bring you some girls, for company?" Gilberto asked somewhat mockingly, while their faces turned red and their eyes grew mischievous.

And so the scoundrel became a matchmaker. A mere signal to Nélida brought her over. After listening to his request, she left the bar and shortly returned with two pretty young girls, barely fourteen or fifteen years old. Upon seeing them, Gilberto stood, brought two stools and invited them to sit. The men stared at each other mutely. Taking up the bottle of , Gilberto served a round of drinks and offered a toast:

"To a day without concerns. Here's to happiness, to friends, and may the girls be very nice to the generals." The conversation soon became very lively. For a long time, the officers shared stories about the army and events in the motherland during the internal political struggles, while the girls pampered them and took over the task of pouring drinks. The officers even told them about how Franco had entered Madrid after he forced the resignation of General José Miaja, president of the Spanish Republican Defense Council.

At three in the morning, the place was practically empty. Gilberto smoked while an overworked jukebox constantly played songs about heartbreak. Nélida gathered dozens of beer and bottles, emptied ashtrays brimming with butts, and wiped down the tables with a rag she rinsed in a bucket of water. Weary from the lateness of the hour and quiet for long minutes, Gilberto held his face in his hands, his elbows propped on the table. The officers and the call girls had left a while earlier.

"Are you planning on staying here? Your elbows will flatten out!" exclaimed Nélida compassionately, looking worn-out from her nightly duties.

"And where am I supposed to go? I have nowhere I should be," replied Gilberto woodenly.

The woman gently caressed his hair and invited him to rest in the small room where the boxes of beer were piled up.

"What happened with the officers?" she asked.

"They're good guys," he said. "They were off-duty and were happy when they left. They were with the girls." Nélida took hold of one of his arms and placed it around her shoulder, though he was able to walk on his own.

"It was nice of you to bring the girls to entertain them, don't you think? So, what did they say about the military service?"

"They didn't actually take me seriously." He took a scrap of paper from his shirt pocket, showing her the two lines written on it: Lieutenant Colonel Stricker; Captain Bonet, Tolemaida battalion. Nélida smiled naughtily. In triumph, Gilberto raised his right eyebrow to underscore his heroism. She unbuttoned his shirt, one button at a time, lowered her hand to his crotch and rubbed him provocatively. Then she picked up her long, lacy skirt, as she did for her customers, and let the young man take her lustily.

Asphalt Coffee

... 1966

It rained all day long in the town of Armenia. It rained so heavily that the neighbors never noticed that some burglars were ransacking the Cervantes' house. The police said that, apparently, nobody had noticed a thing. But according to the daughter of firefighter Ahumada and Doña Inés, some men carried off all the housewares in a rickety old truck. Galilea supposed the family was moving, since there was no fuss. In any case, she didn't pay much attention to the matter, since she couldn't care less about neighbors who never noticed her.

It was Tuesday, Gilberto's day off, which he had used to visit a distant farm. The family's arrival home was beyond sad. Everything had been stolen, even the kitchen things, the children's clothes, and María Sucel's old robe. It was such a bleak scene that Gilberto cried like he did when he was a child and Doña Sara wouldn't let him do whatever he liked. Don Juvenal, who had been out with the family, tried to cheer them up. There wasn't even a sheet left behind, for the thieves had used them to wrap the clothing in bundles. Not even the tube radio to listen to Athletic Quindío games or to the races, or for María Sucel to listen to music while she worked. Not even the iron was spared, nor the white Egyptian cotton shirts that Gilberto wore every day when he went to work at El Marqués, nor the school supplies that the little ones took to Doña Amparo's school. Only one cabinet was left, almost empty. Even the leather sofa where he tickled his children was gone. The crime was so perfect that it must have been carefully planned for a long time.

Galilea gave Gilberto an extremely detailed description of the burglary, urged on by her own father, firefighter Ahumada, who despite being known as a man of few words, was helpful in the face of these circumstances. She described each of the three men she saw removing things from the house. When she detailed that one was rough, copper-skinned, somewhat bald with straight brown hair, and large teeth like a rabbit, Gilberto concluded that it was Ulises.

During the following days, Gilberto felt trapped, and the last thing he wanted was to have to ask Ophir for his money, thinking she might cause another conflict if she revealed everything to his wife. This was what he feared the most, so he was careful to avoid creating any domino effect in his life. He had always been well aware that the woman was mean, and a mean woman scorned was a time bomb that could go off at any moment. Thus, he was forced to choke on his own contradictions and labyrinths. Besides, she had him all confused with her story that the money was in the *Caja Agraria*, in a fixed-term deposit, and apparently a part had been given over to interest and it wouldn't be paid out until the following month. For whatever reason, it was a tangle of lies or truths that kept poor Gilberto steeped in chaos.

As for María Sucel, all she wanted was to recover everything the thieves had taken from the house. She chose to pray, because hope is the last thing one must lose. But passing days diluted that fervor, and they heard nothing back from the police. Thanks to God's miracle, Isabelina said, while she looked towards heaven and crossed herself, still hanging on hooks in the cabinet, undamaged, were the two coats, two white shirts, and black ties that Toñito and Tomás would wear for their First Communion at Sacred Heart church.

María Sucel was engulfed in a depression that had her sleeping fitfully and then startling awake, bathed in a cold sweat. The children were told that their things had been given away to friends and would be replaced with new ones. A convenient explanation for the disappearance of everything in the house, for in that situation, it mattered little if over time they forgot about it and never wondered why the new possessions didn't arrive.

In the days following the looting, Gilberto's siblings Analdo, Dora, and Romelia provided an oil cookstove, two chairs, a wooden table, and even a radio. Isabelina prepared the meals, which she brought over every day in the covered tray that she used to send Elías his lunch. Ruby, a good friend, brought the family some clothing. Gilberto felt a bit calmer. Receiving so many tokens of affection reduced his paranoia. In any case, exhausted by all the bullshit over the money, he became quite disillusioned with Ophir, but he was afraid to get mad at her.

Don Juvenal offered a settlement, in case he needed cash to pull his family from that quagmire. That was very helpful, because he was able to obtain rudimentary furnishings for the house, like cheap furniture for the living room, clothes, and some insignificant household goods. By that point, the thought of escaping from all the crap had lodged in his head, and anything related to Armenia seemed to stink.

The search for renewed fortunes elsewhere obsessed

Gilberto, regardless of whether the places he imagined going to might be remote, or the fact that he knew little or nothing about them. His perception of the big city came only from his own imagination, fueled by passing references and comments heard on the radio, and by the occasional newspaper photograph unfailingly gazed at during recent mornings. The idea of emigrating challenged his esteem, yet aroused his adrenaline. He imagined doing it with a sack over his shoulder, like a snail, or his pack of children clinging to him like marsupials. In any case, with mules packed with crates, along roads as broken as his very own life. It all looked good then. Why not do it, if everything in his life had gone so well this far? He longed to bury his perpetual infidelity under mountains of dirt. All he needed was for Ophir, in an act of genuine solidarity, to hand over the money she held for him, no matter the cost he'd pay for the favor. How ironic!

When Gilberto told María Sucel of his idea to leave Armenia, she didn't think it was that harebrained. At least, not so difficult in comparison with the panic caused by the looting of their home. What did make her sad was the image of her deteriorating father, Elías: decrepit, struggling with a persistent cough that made him irritable and increasingly lonely. She thought of her mother Isabelina: unconditionally loving, diligent, pious, always praying to the most holy Virgin. She imagined her hiding leftover cigarettes in the nooks of the wattle-and-daub walls of her house in the hills of Corbones. María Sucel recalled her wisdom and selflessness and swore to herself to never leave her unprotected. She held on to the hope that her nephew Gabriel, who lived under the same roof, would continue to care for her tired parents, who needed more attention now.

Each day, the idea of leaving to breathe different air was increasingly accepted, more as a fact than as a purpose. There was greater confidence now, because Gilberto, during one of their Sunday chats, had heard from Don Juvenal that far away, across the mountain range, after riding a bus like Don Nacianceno's all day, you arrived in Bogotá, where there were schools and more work, and that was promising. But that wasn't enough for him, because he had heard others say, more realistically, that things in Bogotá wouldn't be easy, what with so many children and his wife giving birth every year. He'd have to work like an animal to support the family. In other words, leaving the countryside—where everything happens with common sense and simplicity—for the big city would be a trial by fire that might burn them all. Gilberto was told that in the big city women had to go to work because there wasn't enough money, and María Sucel had never worked. Another risk was that he didn't know anyone. Well, almost nobody, because Ophir herself told him about someone called Tejada, and his wife.

María Sucel, who was much more naïve, hoped that in the capital her children would be able to advance in life, go to good schools, be surrounded by attention. In any case, this destiny lay ahead of them for better or for worse, according to God's design. It was as the priest had said on their wedding day, when she had committed to being with Gilberto until death, in good times and bad, in sickness and in health. Though she had never imagined that her husband's life would be stormier than the devil.

Gilberto set off on a journey of exploration, his soul full of hope. He went alone, motivated by a desire to find his destiny and learn to handle whatever life in the capital would bring. He hoped there would be schools for his children as well as good friends for the family and many opportunities for happiness. Everyone's life could be improved by setting up a business with the savings that Ophir was holding, plus whatever was left from the sale of the house and his coffee plantations on his neighbors' property.

Only two days into Gilberto's stay in frigid Bogotá, María Sucel began to suffer from vomiting and an aversion to the smell of certain spices. She was once again pregnant. If it was a boy, they would call him Acacio Elías, like both grandfathers, and, if a girl, they would call her Sara Isabelina, like both grandmothers. It was a kind of tribute they had agreed on months earlier in the event she had another pregnancy. According to happy calculations, the birth would be in March or April of '67. At the time, October '66, the Cervantes Baroja family already numbered eight: six children plus the two of them. They celebrated the news, though for María Sucel it was a weary enthusiasm; at barely twenty-eight she considered herself drained by motherhood.

Maria Sucel was exhausted. Her belly grew every time, for the enjoyment of Gilberto, whom she didn't want to reject. She wanted to rebel against God and the Church, but when she saw that almost all the women in the neighborhood and the city had ten or twelve children, she kept silent. Her self-denial was such that she didn't even express her mutinous feelings. One day she had tried to suggest the idea of avoiding more pregnancies to Isabelina, and got scolded to the point that she felt she deserved excommunication. According to the priests at San Francisco, babies could not be avoided because they were signs of divine grace, and so preached Pope Paul VI to the whole world.

When he returned from Bogotá a month later, Gilberto

learned of the pregnancy and was filled with joy. This would be their first rolo, which is what they call people from Bogotá. The child would be born smelling of beans and *almojábana* buns, for those born in Armenia, he said, were steeped in coffee. After a few days, he began to spread the word among close acquaintances about the sale of the house in El Paraíso and to request his settlement from El Marqués. Those funds, plus what Ophir was holding, would help them put down roots in their voluntary exile in the country's capital. Neither the Cervantes nor the Baroja family were familiar with Santa Fe de Bogotá or with the breadth of its complexities. They had never imagined that they would have a second life there or that their experience would so abruptly morph from the civility of country neighbors in their native homeland to the pollution of the city, with its hostile crowds of mistrusting people who didn't even greet one another.

Curious for news from Ophir, he knocked on her door and waited. He knocked three times before asking the landlord, who lived in the same building, about her. The man told him that she had vacated the apartment and had left sporting a bruised face, a broken arm, and a dislocated shoulder. He said a man had pushed his way into Ophir's apartment and the landlord only realized what was happening when he heard all the noise, which ended with the guy breaking the door as he left. He told Gilberto he had been afraid to get involved and that it seemed that the guy was someone she knew, because she had not wanted to say anything about what had happened. *It must have been that bastard Ulises,* Gilberto thought indignantly.

"The shouting was so loud even the neighbors came out, concerned," the landlord added. "The whole mess lasted over an hour, until the man charged out like a crazy person. I thought he was going to kill her. When we ran in to help her, she was whimpering but not crying. She was almost unconscious, breathless, and moaning from the pain."

"What did the guy look like?" Gilberto asked.

"He was a very strange-looking man, kind of dark and with his teeth sticking out," he replied. That was when Gilberto definitely linked him to Ulises.

Ophir had now been gone for a couple of weeks and, according to the owner of the apartment, before leaving she had paid everything she owed. She had left everything behind, without another word. Gilberto recalled her asking for time to forget him and to get used to the idea that she wouldn't die if he was no longer there—maybe a few months, or a few years. But he also thought perhaps she had run away to protect herself from Ulises. Confused, he struggled to put two and two together. Gilberto remembered that she had asked him not to visit her so often, until she had reached the point where she no longer needed to see him—until she could forget him, without it hurting so much. He remembered Ophir telling him that one day he would come and she would no longer be waiting for him. And despite all those premonitions and warnings, he had not done what was needed to secure the money.

Faced with so much drama, Gilberto collapsed. Desperate, he sold the house in Armenia, along with the coffee plantations and everything, and received a significant sum with which to start the merchandise business in Bogotá with Don Octavio Tejada. He had committed himself to buying home furnishings at wholesale prices and envisioned that an army of traveling salesmen provided by Don Octavio would help to sell them in popular neighborhoods in the city, in instalments and at a 200 percent yield in one year, after which he would be able to manage his business with his own crew.

The die was cast. The following day, very early, they would leave for Bogotá. The suitcases and bundles were ready, and all that was left to be done was to get the children ready and go. Gilberto had hidden away a small amount of money as a reserve, in a paper bag stashed inconspicuously in the headboard of the bed they would be taking. He would carry most of their small fortune in a briefcase that he kept near him even when going to the bathroom.

Their departure was imminent, and the friends shared their condolences as if attending a funeral. Isabelina knew that her goodbyes would be sad and heartfelt, all the more so when it came time to bless each of the eight individuals who were facing this exile that she found so perplexing. The parents and the "little ones," as she called them, were at the core of her joy in living. Grandfather Elías grieved, but he had hope. He had faith that the distance would restore dignity to his loved ones' home. Although it had been a long time since he had thought about God, because he simply forgot, he asked Him to accompany María Sucel and light her way. He also asked Isabelina to say a prayer in his name.

María Sucel couldn't hide her regret at leaving her parents, especially now that they were so old. Her eyes were red from so much crying for days, still damp from the anguish she carried in her soul. She thought to offer her father some coffee as a last gesture, to thank him for making her happy since the day she was born. Glad to have a few moments alone together, he watched her quietly preparing it before suddenly scolding her: "Daughter, you should not be sad."

María Sucel spun around with tear-filled eyes. Swallowing

hard, she ran to embrace her father, who wept as old folks do, with less drama and completely seriously. Neither wished to end the embrace, until finally she was able to say, "I'll miss you two so much."

Elías couldn't respond; the lump in his throat made it impossible. His daughter, however, offered him coffee.

"In all my twenty-eight years, it's the first time that we will be apart for more than a day, and it breaks my heart," she said.

"Remember us always as the two people who love you the most and will miss you the most," answered Elías, taking her hands in his, somewhat comforted by her sorrow. "When I am gone, I only ask that you not forsake Isabelina, and should fate allow you to attend my burial, bring a flower to throw on my casket before the dirt is piled over it. That will please me." María Sucel embraced the old man again. She sensed that his words foreshadowed sad days for everyone. She placed a heartfelt kiss on his unshaven cheek and wiped away the tears flowing from his eyes with her fingertips.

"I will keep you in my prayers and will teach the children to follow your example. We will remember you as two wonderful people. I feel so proud of being a Baroja Sanchez and to have witnessed your days as camp supervisor. Your character, and your zeal. Your kindness ..." Elías kissed her hands and then her forehead.

"Give the children a kiss from me and a hug for your husband." He coughed as he turned and walked away. María Sucel's eyes followed him as he slowly shuffled along. Though he was weak and sick, he was beautiful to her. Deeply moved, she silently blessed him. Knowing Elías, she knew that once he had made the decision to leave, he wouldn't turn around to look at her again. María Sucel dried her tears and remembered the days of careful restrictions during the '50s. She reflected on the ironies of life, which can be so intense even though so much depends on mundane circumstances. Joy, she reflected, was always accompanied by suffering, and pain was a bridge to rewards; even if those rewards weren't realized, hope that they would come remained the most solid incentive to go on. What saddened her the most now was the feeling that, to seek stability elsewhere, she was leaving behind the ones who needed her most.

Bearing her sadness silently, Isabelina was preparing baby bottles and diaper bags for the trip when María Sucel approached to say goodbye. "My father has already said goodbye," she said plaintively.

Isabelina smiled sadly but said nothing for a moment. She knew the time had come to express how much she would miss them, now that a huge piece of her soul was leaving with them, taking with it much of her reason to live. She also knew her "Marujita," as she affectionately called María Sucel, was suffering as much as she was. Isabelina felt she should speak first.

"Pray these novenas for the children to remain healthy, and though they are small books, the letters are big so you can read them. This other one is so that your marriage is always filled with happiness, as it has been until now. This is to ask God that Gilberto always have work. In any case, I wrote down what each one of them is for. Remember, daughter, that before you pray you must light a candle to the Virgin and bless yourself."

"I know, Mother. Thank you, and God bless you also, and my father and Gabriel."

Isabelina arranged the package with novenas in one of the

compartments of the suitcase, making sure that her daughter could find them easily.

"I have a feeling that your leaving will be forever and that my last days with Elías will be lonely," said Isabelina. "I feel that my hope of growing old near my grandchildren will languish over the hours, the days, and the years, and that with this farewell the image of their grandmother will only be a lovely memory in the distance, like a story about someone who loves them very much but will not enjoy them for the rest of their lives. I will keep my memories, and hold in my heart the dream that one day I will see them again, and in my spirit the hope that God will grant them long and exemplary lives."

María Sucel listened in silence, touched and helpless in the face of her mother's great humility. She wanted to run away from that painful reality but embraced her instead. She put her arms around her as she sobbed.

"Your grandchildren will grow up loving you both and speaking proudly about you for generations to come. They will want to see you, and we will bring them whenever we can, as many times as necessary, and you will also visit us whenever you want, no matter that we will be on the other side of the mountains," she declared as she held her. Thus they shared their advice for each other, exchanging beautiful words with knots in their throats.

"Write to me sometimes," said Isabelina, trying to be brave and inwardly taking into account that María Sucel was pregnant. To bring this painful exercise to an end, Isabelina drew a smile on her face with a pencil she dug out from a hidden corner of her soul.

Gilberto and María Sucel finished saying their goodbyes to everyone who, until that first day of February 1967, had made their days in El Paraiso more comfortable, in each corner of the city they were leaving behind. The bus, one equipped for long journeys, would leave at six in the morning.

Only minutes before the departure, when they were all seated and anxious about our farewells and last view of Elías and Isabelina, Ulises and two other thugs surrounded Gilberto outside the bus, threatening him with a gun and snatching the briefcase with the money, without anyone else noticing. "Get on the bus, you stupid asshole, and keep quiet or we'll kill you and your wife. Do you want your children to become orphans so young? And don't even think about coming back here, because at the very least your wife will find out what kind of husband she has."

That was checkmate for the king, and for all his family. Right there they lost the game of their own lives. Gilberto thought Ulises and Ophir were the evil that led to his undoing—that truly finished him off. Overcoming his extreme despair and disappointment, he managed to get on the bus, putting on a cheerful and enthusiastic act with María Sucel while desperately trying to think of what he could do in the next minutes—seconds, really—to recover the money, which was truly impossible.

The intercity bus departed, carrying the eight of us as we peered through the windows, waving, fearfully facing the unknown. Engraved in the travelers' minds was the sweet sight of Isabelina's slight figure going to pray at San Francisco, wrapped in her shawl.

Gilberto had barely exhaled after our departure when he realized that there were still some remnants of his fortune stored below in the bus, and he breathed a sigh of slight relief. But then his head drooped as he was again overcome by sadness. His eyes passed across his children's faces; he looked again at his wife, took her hand and kissed it. Feeling tender and pious, she crossed herself and did the same toward each of her little ones. Then she blessed Gilberto and said, "God protect us."

It was a long trip, overflowing with expectations, and awe at the valleys and ravines the bus passed through. A trip with stops for cold meat and much childish banter, the children's attention distracted by cars along the road and by people in the towns who approached to offer *manjar blanco* and cheesecake in packs of a hundred, or some peach-palm fruit or chunks of pineapple or cold oats. He pretended to be excited to keep them all cheerful, which made María Sucel happy and helped her deal with pregnancy-related indigestion and nausea during the trip. Gilberto thought and thought about what to do with his family adrift, as they neared the cold and left behind the warmth of Armenia. He assumed that the money stored in the bed would only be enough to partly cover his commitment to Don Octavio and that perhaps he wouldn't be able to afford that nice house he had verbally agreed on. Nevertheless, he said nothing to María Sucel, so as not to distress her. He thought he might be able to persuade the truck driver he'd hired to wait for them with their stuff and take them somewhere decent.

At about two in the afternoon, the bus arrived in a grey Santa Fe de Bogotá that welcomed them with a persistent drizzle and intense cold. Gilberto had managed to locate the truck driver who would transport, in his small vehicle, their few belongings and the heavy bed where the new baby would be born and others would be created. There wasn't much in their luggage, mostly clothing and kitchen things. Just as with Don Naciancheno's once-endearing bus, the one that had brought them to Bogotá became a thing of the past once they had disembarked and stood huddled together on the cold street at the bus terminal. The mother tried to shelter the children while she kept her eyes on their belongings, exactly as Gilberto had told her to do when he warned that thieves wandered about in that vicinity, adding that they were much more aggressive than the ones in Quindío. Fortunately, he was soon back and comforted them.

Gilberto asked María Sucel to let him speak to the trucker for a few short minutes. That was when she asked him about the briefcase with the money. So, he was forced to tell her that some thugs with a gun had stolen it as they were leaving Armenia, and that he had chosen not to tell her to avoid ruining her trip. He also told her that they only had what was hidden in the bed. The tragedy of this now overwhelmed them. She went into shock, unable to say a word and looking sluggish, as if she had been drugged. She wondered, what wrongs they had done to deserve such terrible punishment?

The truck had been circling through neighborhoods that clearly proved they were immersed in a city much larger than Armenia, with a huge number of newer and prettier buses than Don Nacianceno's, and with many people dressed in thick, dark clothing to ward off the cold. Not even Gilberto, who had already been to Bogotá, knew where the driver was taking them, and he dared not ask. The truth is that the man looked tough as well as worried. He took them to a place, God knows why, that seemed to him the best, according to what Gilberto had told him in confidence regarding their situation since leaving Armenia. A seedy rooming house he knew of, maybe somewhere he had lived himself.

Located in a working-class area, it was a three-story house

with a rooftop terrace, across the street from a certain Don Alirio's bakery, in the heart of a neighborhood called La Granja. It was built of red bricks, without a single plant outside to relieve the concrete that covered the whole area like a train platform. To everyone's surprise, about fourteen families lived there, sharing a single laundry room and one bathroom per floor. The place felt disconcerting and unsafe, especially to María Sucel, who could not hide her dissatisfaction once she realized that this was to be their new home. She was terrified by the dirt on the walls and the excessive hardware on the main entrance, with four bars across the only door everyone used—as though she was beginning a sentence in an urban prison where all the inmates were people like her, with children and a husband.

    A beaten Gilberto negotiated for a while with the owner of the place and then led them to a large room with a green-tinted cement floor and whitewashed walls that seemed grayish due to the gloom. As it was tucked well within the center of the house, the room seemed especially sad. The only beam of natural light came from a window with four lattices, about 25 centimeters each, that looked out over a central patio where the tenants' youngest children played. Once inside, he asked them to wait while he arranged the suitcases and other things, with the assistance of a man who came out of one of the apartments and kindly offered to help. María Sucel appreciated this noble gesture, and for a moment she forgot about the cold and the uncertainty. Nevertheless, she soon felt depressed once more and even thought to demand a home more like the one she'd known all her life. But she kept quiet, in silent remorse for bringing her children to such a crowded, cold place.

    "This is where we'll live!" exclaimed Gilberto, panting from the exertion of putting together the bed. "You and I will sleep on the bed, with Sarita and Cesarino; Maru and Piedad will sleep on this daybed, and the older ones will sleep on top of the suitcases filled with clothes. We'll be uncomfortable tonight, but I'll purchase some heavy quilts and blankets made of virgin wool. Did you know, dear, that this is the land of sheep, and their wool is used to make clothing to combat the cold?"

"I never thought we would live this way," was all she could think of saying.

He looked at her and was silent, understanding that there would never emerge in her grieving face a hint of resignation. Holding his hands out to her and hunching his shoulders, he tried to explain his plans.

"It will only be until I can find a more suitable house. For now, we must understand the most important thing—that we're together, and we'll live together for all eternity. Together we'll move forward. Besides, we still have the money we brought hidden in the bed. How would it be, dear, if we used that little bit of cash on a fancy house? What would we live on while we learn to live in this Bogotá? I beg the Lord not to let discouragement overtake us so quickly. Let's be patient, just for a few days. You'll see, things will get better. I know that many people live in this house and that they are poor, humble people, who have never had anything, but from these people we will learn how to live in this city."

"Let's go back to Armenia, dear," she begged him. Gilberto searched deep inside himself for another lie—that is, another truth—so powerful that it could make his wife stop wishing to return to Armenia and push her to start fighting for a future in the big city. He reminded her of the great opportunities the family would have in a city where the children would be able to study and advance, a city where so many rural people from around the country were arriving to get a new start in their lives. But this reasoning did not convince María Sucel. So, Gilberto pushed on with a new confession—a forceful, surprising, or sly one. He needed to diffuse the tremendous impact the earlier robbery had had on him, somehow, so he wouldn't burst from carrying the trauma of it alone.

"Honey, I didn't want to tell you earlier, but promise you'll stay calm about it." She looked at him, quietly subdued, giving him a certain calmness in which he could explain.

"Those bastards who robbed me were very clear, threatening that if I returned, they would hurt us all, even you and the children. It seemed that they knew me and were following me," he added. "Nothing in the world would make me risk our family's safety. My dear, let us be patient, for God's sake. The children are very small and they'll adapt. So will we, because we are older and grown up." With her usual compliance, María Sucel reluctantly heeded his pleas as she stood, unmoving, with little Cesarino in her arms. She tucked some wayward strands of hair behind her ears, understanding that there was nothing more to say in the midst of arriving and settling in with all their belongings. She walked to a corner of the room and laid the boy down on the scarf she had been wearing. Gilberto quietly approached her from behind and whispered into her ear, trying to help her recover her trust in him.

"For today, don't suffer," Gilberto said. "Help me make this situation less difficult. The only sin committed by the families who live here is that of being poor. But they will help us learn their habits for living in this huge and complex city. Armenia is paradise, we know that. Our dear paradise is so beautiful, like our family. We will never forget what we had there with our neighbors. But here, too, we'll go far. Don't be so easily discouraged. I'm sure that all the liveliness of our family will bring warmth to these walls. And besides, when our first batch of sugarcane panela is boiling in this old house, the aroma will attract everyone's friendship. Our neighbors will help us learn something useful every day to get us rolling toward our children's destiny. Please forgive me for asking you to make this sacrifice."

Gilberto was begging her to understand. He was facing the first real crisis of his life, one in which his wife and children were involved, or even worse, directly affected. They were speaking quietly so they wouldn't upset the children, although the little ones were oblivious to any feelings, happy or unhappy, and were shyly getting to know the other children who had come, timidly and curiously, to greet them.

Although Gilberto was possibly the one who had been most battered by these events, he knew that he had to do what he could to raise María Sucel's low spirits. He had never thought she would express such dissatisfaction. He tried again to whisper pitifully and lovingly in her ear.

"You know how much I love you. As long as we're together, everything will be wonderful. Who cares if we look like a bunch of newly arrived mountain people? With so many people all around us, loneliness won't stand a chance of damaging our spirits. In a few days, or maybe a few hours, we'll have learned at least a little about their customs. We'll learn things that will be useful when we go to live on our own. Knowing how cheerful and enterprising you've always been, I figured it would be better if you were surrounded by people while I go out to make a living. In a few days, you'll have made friends with some of the neighbors, and the children will be playing with the others in the patio, you'll see." She listened to him without saying a word and without taking her eyes off her little ones as they jumped around with their peers.

A few hours later, after much rearranging, things felt less crowded than they had at first. In the kitchen, in a small pot on a pressurized-fuel stove temporarily borrowed from a neighbor woman, Gilberto warmed up some foamy chocolate, which he whipped with the old beater they had brought from Armenia, and they drank it with some fresh, warm parva pastries from Don Alirio's bakery.

On the night of that fateful day, their energy was exhausted by nine o'clock. The crowded family spent the night under many warm blankets to deal with the freezing cold. As always, María Sucel enjoyed the warmth of her husband's protective arms under the virgin wool.

The following day, the children's cheeks were reddened, and their concerned mother tried to keep their runny noses wiped clean. One of the neighbors told her that on the high plateau, runny noses were a common thing among children, not something to worry about as long as there were no signs of fever or other cold symptoms. This timely explanation made María Sucel think about the knowledge her new neighbors would provide, and she partly believed what Gilberto had said the day before. Over the following days, new characters were added to the lives of these newcomers to the asphalt. Don Antonio, the robust storeowner on the corner, who sold food and grain to the neighborhood at inflated resale prices; the Pinto family, who sold fresh, foamy milk and brown eggs at a good price out of a makeshift garage a couple of blocks away, farm products that arrived every day at dawn from the Bogotá savannah, together with the newspapers; and the Velarde family, who ran the only butcher shop and were open every day until seven at night.

In times of Hitler and other things

...1939

"Boss! Boss! Is nine million a lot, boss?" a worker named Asdrúbal asked Elías one September morning as he coordinated some demolition work.

Surprised and more than a little curious, Elías responded with a wrinkled brow. "That would depend, Asdrúbal, on what we're talking about. If you're referring to how many rocks we've broken up as we clear the way for roads, I'd say it's not too many. Now, if we're talking about—"

"They said on the radio that there are nine million of us living in Colombia, but they didn't say whether it was a lot or a little," Asdrúbal explained.

"I'd say it's not a lot, for this land is vast and generous," Elías replied, with no further explanation. "Fortunately, there are opportunities here for everyone. There is no fighting in Colombia, like there is in Europe." With practiced subtlety, he urged the man to go back to work alongside the others, who were breaking rocks and sweating as they mixed cement to pour into the wooden frames that shaped the edges of the road.

Approximately every thirty minutes, the air shook with the sound of detonations. Large rocks were masterfully blown apart by Eliseo Soto, a blue-eyed man about Elías's age, who usually worked alone. They all admired him for his dedication and his stern personality, and nobody knew if he had any family. The whole crew depended on his work, for he was the only dynamiter in the region and made it possible for the road construction to move forward. Eliseo always worked a kilometer ahead of the main work site; there, he would mark the explosion guides, and then gather his sharp chisels and mallets to open dozens of holes, into which he would capably stuff the dynamite sticks and their corresponding fuses. He was a meticulous man by nature; he could never otherwise have handled such danger. Therefore, he never got drunk or went carousing. Eliseo behaved like a hermit who only knew how to do one thing but did it well. That morning he arrived and, as usual, he reported to Elías, doffing his hat as he greeted the supervisor.

"How are you, Eliseo? What's new?" asked Elías without looking at him.

"Man, Don Elías ... life moves along, but you never know where it's headed. The world is in such an uproar that I find detonating the charges much less terrifying than the news. I do it to blow up rocks, but the Germans are advancing ferociously and setting off detonations to destroy their fellow man," he said thoughtfully and sadly. "How ironic! The world never stops struggling," he added, pressing his lips together. "It is said that Hitler is personally advancing using a strategy that worked wonderfully for the Germans in 1914. Apparently, it's called 'blitzkrieg.' I know this because every morning, when I leave my house, I walk by the corner store and chat with a neighbor—he's military and knowledgeable about European things. Hmm ... I don't think this war will leave anything behind but despair across the land," he said. "According to him, the offensive strategy allowed Hitler to occupy one hundred kilometers along the border of Saarland and the central section of the Rhine. That would be a very big battle!

"By the way, Don Elías. Have you heard that we are nine million souls living in this beloved Colombia?" asked Eliseo. Elías nodded and shouted for two black coffees.

"Asdrúbal came to me about it this morning, asking me whether nine million was a lot or a little. How about that? That Asdrúbal is funny."

"Doesn't he know what the numbers mean?" Eliseo asked quickly.

"The man can barely sign his name! We're being overrun by numbers. Do you know, Eliseo, that in 1800 our population was two million, and in one hundred years we became four million, which means our population doubled. And in the last forty years, we're already more than nine million people."

Eliseo took a deep breath and stretched his neck, relaxing his shoulders. "We're like rabbits and don't even realize it," he declared as he exhaled. "At this rate we'll definitely have to dynamite rocks, because the number of people coming through here is going to be huge."

Elías was lost in thought, imagining the situation in Europe. He thought about Isabelina and his daughters. He shivered to think about the things that were happening, which he sensed could have an effect on his life. He picked up the paper, eager to read news about events that concerned him. He spent long minutes reading attentively about the impending war in Europe, about events related to the Soviet occupation of eastern Poland, even about the death of Sigmund Freud, whom many ignorant people called frivolous, but whom he considered an example of thoroughgoing empiricism. One news item he always looked for carefully addressed coffee prices in New York, which had suffered a drop, though they were still holding at promising levels. He remained thoughtful, without interrupting his work. The news and his little daughters' faces filtered through his mind. He pondered Eliseo's words that the German's explosive advances foretold stormy times for the whole area. He worried that road construction would be halted someday due to a lack of foreign investments, or maybe because the country would also go to war in support of an ally or a country it owed favors to. What he didn't know was who Colombia owed its loyalty to, and what payment that loyalty would extract from the simple society in which he lived.

He finished organizing some papers and spoke politely to Asdrúbal, saying, "Please find a young man— I'm not sure if he's from Salamina or Neira, but he must be in one of the cafés along the way. His name is Gilberto Cervantes-Cervantes. Ask him to come by the construction site. Tell him it's on behalf of Elías, the man he met in church at his little girl's baptism."

After washing Elías's white shirts, Isabelina soaked them in cassava starch before pressing them with a heavy iron, which she heated with charcoal. Her young daughters played nearby with dolls she had made for them herself with bits of old clothes and her husband's old socks. In between housework and caring for the girls, she fixed her husband's wool trousers, ironing them impeccably. Her motto was, "a well-dressed husband is the sign of an irreproachable wife at home." According to her parents, women were responsible for a family's image; men, for the hardiness of its members.

Happiness came into their home every time Elías arrived back in Salamina from his far-off workplaces. Isabelina would have a large bowl of hot water waiting for him, and she would make him sit down in a heavy chair. She'd pull off his shoes and socks, so he could soak his tired feet to get some relief. For him, the most important thing was to hold María Sucel in his arms, relishing this moment of peace while fending off his daughters' jealousy. Isabelina found any excuse she could to pop delicious tidbits into his mouth as she prepared dinner.

That evening, once they were in bed and under the covers, Elías told her that he had sent Asdrúbal to find Gilberto because he wanted to offer him an administrative job in the construction site's office. He needed an assistant to help him with ordering supplies and preparing the payroll. They chatted about having noticed something special about the young man and both thought that, despite having been beaten down by life, he was harmless. Nevertheless, despite Asdrúbal's efforts to locate him, they never heard from Gilberto, and they slowly forgot about him.

The little girls grew, and the entire family returned to the construction site, and harmony reigned. Isabelina once again coordinated all the household chores with precision, and the morning routine resumed the hectic pace it had known before she delivered her baby.

One morning in October 1942, Isabelina traveled to Manizales to buy some supplies for the site, since Elías was suffering a bad cold they were treating with goose-fat poultices on his chest. She was accompanied by trusted workers he had assigned to the task after breakfast and was in the site's van by 9 a.m. It was a sunny day, like almost every other day in that area, splendidly revealing a perfect communion between earth and sky. The noise was deafening, the van rumbling with the effort of trying to gain traction on the steep slopes towards Manizales. Otherwise, it was a silent trip; Isabelina kept her eyes forward without saying a word. As the supervisor's wife, having undertaken a solitary errand, it would be considered unseemly for her to start a conversation with the men escorting her. It was a winding road, and mostly unpaved. The monotony was broken when the worker sitting on the right leaned over to look in the vehicle's rearview mirror. He did it several times and then was still, his eyes steady.

"Is something wrong, young man?" asked Isabelina.

The worker scratched his nose, concerned about being certain of what he saw before speaking.

"I'm not sure, ma'am, but I think that's an army truck behind us."

Isabelina turned her head and confirmed what the worker thought he saw. The van left a thick curtain of dust behind it that impeded a clear view of the vehicle in its wake, and although she tried to identify it further, she preferred to continue keeping her eyes forward. Cars were not her specialty, and even less those used by the authorities. They continued on their way, and about a half hour later, a dark green truck began to pass them. The back had open wooden sides and was driven by soldiers. As it passed, it threw up a lot of dust that filtered into the van. Their driver and the other worker hurried to shut the windows as Isabelina covered her mouth to avoid breathing in the pervasive dust. Isabelina was curious about the army recruiters that everyone was so afraid of.

"Is that an army truck?" she asked.

"Yes, ma'am, it's full of young men that they're taking to Manizales."

As the truck passed them on the left, they could see about twenty young men gripping tightly to the wood slats to brace themselves against the rough movements caused by the road's uneven surface. There were eight stern-faced soldiers with them, carrying rifles, who didn't even turn to look at the van or its occupants. Captivated by the scene, Isabelina noted the sadness in the young men's faces, their hair covered in a film of dust picked up during their journey.

"And where are they taking them?"

"To the army," they chimed in.

"They are new recruits for the battalion," one of them added nervously.

Isabelina understood the detainees' despair and felt fortunate for not having sons. The drama of these young men touched her deeply, and she understood how their families were suffering. As the truck passed them and began to move towards the right to take its place in front of the van, Isabelina silently looked at each of the young men's faces in turn. One specifically caught her attention when he turned towards the van, startled by a noise from the struggling engine. He was on the right side of the truck, next to two other men, but not standing like the others. Isabelina saw misery in his face. In a moment, the dust once again hid the image of those powerless men, and she linked her hands together and whispered a prayer.

"Don't distress yourself, Doña Isabelina, it might do you harm," the driver exclaimed compassionately. She looked at him wordlessly, and then looked forward again, trying to see into the truck ahead, her eyes wide open and full of tears. She covered her mouth, and two large tears rolled down her cheeks as a quiet moan of pain and despair escaped her throat. She was transfixed by that young man's battered, bloody face as he silently crouched there in the truck.

For a few seconds their eyes met again, and the young man stood up when he apparently recognized her and realized that she was looking at him with sympathy. As soon as he got to his feet, a soldier hit him in the face and stomach with the butt of his rifle. The young man rolled on the floor of the truck and was immediately set upon by four other soldiers and their rifle butts.

Isabelina cried to herself as she watched the truck speed away, taking the battered face with it. Something told her the young man had recognized her, but she couldn't pin down her own memory of him. She tried to place that face with the sons of the women at the construction site, but that didn't help. It was all confusing. For the rest of the trip, she continued to search her memory. Upon arriving in Manizales, she asked the driver to take her to the cathedral, wanting to pray and dispel her despair. Walking towards the altar, she arranged the scarf she had brought on her head.

"Lord, take pity on those who suffer," she prayed softly. "Our Father, who art in heaven, look towards him and help him." Looking at the statue of Our Lady of Mount Carmel, she prayed for them all and for her family. Isabelina called upon God and thought of the face of the young man from the truck, trying again to identify him. She searched her memory, letting her eyes roam over each detail of the cathedral. As she prepared to leave, she thought for a moment of María Sucel and her most precious moments. Suddenly, her face filled with panic as she recognized the similarities between that young man's eyes and the gray ones belonging to the handsome young man who had picked up María Sucel's pacifier on the day she was baptized.

Mutely, alone in the cathedral, Isabelina wept, trying to calm herself enough to go outside, where her escorts were waiting. She dried her tears so they wouldn't notice. She asked the driver to make the necessary purchases on her behalf and assured him she would meet them at the same place in a couple of hours. Going back inside the cathedral, Isabelina took a candle and lit others placed in front of Our Lady of Perpetual Help, and prayed quietly for twenty minutes. Getting to her feet, she crossed herself and walked out, turning once to look again at the main altar and kneeling to cross herself before leaving.

It was a sunny day, though the cold air coming down from the stark Nevado del Ruiz volcano brushed softly against Isabelina's face. Visitors to the plaza were shopping nearby, and on the street, riders and horse-drawn carriages mingled with a few cars; most of the women in the surrounding area were accompanied by their husbands. She walked along the sidewalk slowly, without knowing where she was headed. She knew that, in any case, she would not go beyond the limits of the plaza, for she could not enter an area closed to respectable women.

As she wandered among the passersby, her mind was filled with the image of that young man's face, feeling even greater despair now that he was no longer a mysterious unknown person to her. *My Lord, what keeps us linked to this person who comes and goes from our lives so briefly? Should we help him? Is this what you want, God, or do you want to make a man out of him with bitter, painful experiences? I don't know what to think. Help me, Lord, to not fill my head any longer with painful obligations towards unknown people; help me not to be so profoundly human; help me not to think of him, with his battered face and his eyes begging for help,* she prayed silently, as she desperately but fruitlessly searched for someone she could approach to start a conversation about military matters. As she walked along, she spotted a military vehicle in which rode two men dressed in camouflage uniforms. She followed it, walking quickly to keep it in sight. The truck turned into the plaza and parked in front of a store selling fabric and imported cloth. The military men got out of the vehicle and entered the store. Isabelina ran more than a block and rushed inside. There they were. She took a moment to calm herself after the run and used a delicate handkerchief to wipe the sweat from her forehead and chin.

When she approached him, the storekeeper said, "I'll be with you in a minute."

"Don't worry, sir," she replied, indicating that, though he had lovely fabric for sale, all she needed was to speak to the army men. The store owner drew back, a look of understanding on his face. Isabelina approached the men and asked them respectfully about where the army recruits were to be taken.

"To any battalion in the country," one of them replied, boastful of his power.

Days later, quietly, Elías got on the bus and rode a

long while until he arrived at the café district in Salamina. Entering one of the bars, he sat and ordered a beer and a pack of cigarettes. At 9 a.m., the place was more or less full, and most of the groups of people sitting at the tables were drinking coffee. He asked the waiter for a book of matches and then asked him if he knew Gilberto. The man scratched his chin and raised his eyebrows, trying to link the name to a face, finally answering negatively. Elías insisted, describing him as a young man, about twenty years old, well dressed, with curly hair and a mustache, who was often at the cafés. The man thought for a while, repeating the name to himself, and as he couldn't recall him, urged Elías to visit the bars around the plaza and return later in the afternoon, around 3 p.m., when the ladies of the night began their shift. Elías sipped his beer and, after finishing it, paid and left. After several coffees and beers in various places, he gave up and headed toward the municipal offices to take care of some errands.

Mediums and Spirits

...*1967*

The postman knocked on the door so forcefully, following it with an ear-splitting whistle and a cry of "letter for Isabelina Sánchez," that Isabelina almost dropped to the floor with a heart attack. But once she realized that it was the postman, she exchanged her alarm for the sweet feeling of having news from her daughter, who was so far away. She smiled as she hurried to open the door, so the postman wouldn't break down her door.

"Hello, I'm Isabelina Sánchez," she said, holding out her hand excitedly.

The postman took hold of the pen he had stashed behind his right ear. He was riding a sturdy bicycle, one of those with mud guards on the wheels, a bell and a horn on the handlebars, and a plastic box strapped on the back fender. Without responding, he took his delivery form and scribbled something on it before handing Isabelina the letter and taking off downhill.

Isabelina was so overcome with happiness that she kissed the envelope when she confirmed that it was from her daughter, whom she hadn't heard from since the day she'd left. She tore it open along its left side, taking care not to damage the sender's address, as she sat on the bed under the dim light of a 25-watt bulb screwed into a short lead, which they also used to power the iron and the radio. That bulb, which was also their ceiling lamp despite creating more shadows than illumination, was often the only company the two old people shared during their lonely days. However, its dimness was what she wanted, for she guessed that excessive light made Elías's head ache. He spent most of his time lying down and coughing, when he wasn't sitting on a stool on their patio looking out over the city. She quickly found her glasses on the night table, put them on, and excitedly read the letter.

Bogotá, June 3, 1967

Dear Mother: I hope that this letter finds you well, and my father and Gabriel too. The baby has been born and just as we had discussed, we've named him Acasio Elías, though a young orphan girl that we took in from the street called Rosalía, who helps me with housework and laundry, has nicknamed him Chinche, maybe because he's small. The child is beautiful and no trouble, as he sleeps well at night. The boys and girls are thrilled with him. We've moved three times so far, always in the same neighborhood because it's near the school the children are attending. We are now living in a small separate apartment with two rooms and a bathroom, and we're more organized than at first, when we arrived at an uncomfortable rooming house because Gilberto had miscalculated and money doesn't go far here, you can imagine what we went through but don't worry because my God is great. We have met good people who have offered us their friendship and affection. Gilberto started working with a country couple who own a restaurant and a business that sells home furnishings from pushcarts, he is a salesman on the streets now. Something like the avocado or salt fish vendors that go by every morning shouting their wares. Well, the only difference is that Gilberto doesn't shout, he walks and knocks on doors. Thanks to God and your prayers, he

has done well because he works five hours a day walking around the city offering the merchandise to housewives who buy it with payment plans. The worst is that he walks the streets all the time, pushing a heavy iron cart with four metal wheels where he carries wool blankets, sweaters, bedclothes, aluminum pots, tableware and other things, upon request. On Saturdays and Sundays, he collects payments, pedaling a large black bicycle that is heavier than even our bed, and as you know he's so well-oriented that he already is familiar with Bogotá from walking from one end to the other. I have missed you both very much, especially for the food that you prepared, your daily visits, and all the love you gave us. Please write and tell me how my father is and everyone I know. Expect another letter from your loving daughter who misses you. A kiss for you and a hug for my father and for Gabriel as well. Give my regards to Ruby, to my mother-in-law and sisters-in-law. Tell them everything I've told you and give them my address, so they can also write to me. Kisses ...
María Sucel

Isabelina took off her glasses, closed her eyes and took a deep breath, releasing it together with the stress she'd been carrying from not hearing from her faraway daughter. Walking to the patio where Elías was resting, she gave him the letter excitedly, saying with a smile, "This will make you happy."

Intrigued, Elías held out his hand and asked, "What's this, my dear?"

"Just read it," she replied. "You'll like it."

Elías read the first few lines. He smiled uncertainly, and to be sure, he asked, "A letter from our Marujita?"

"How about that, dear? She says they are well. But, please, before you begin reading, please show me which way is Bogotá?" Elías's forehead wrinkled in thought. His wife had been asking for days about the location of the capital, in order to send blessings in that direction, assuming that, praying in that way, God would be more merciful on the now-exiled coffee growers. She also repeatedly asked about the location of Manizales in order to pray for Bertha, who was married to Eliseo, and about Salento, a town in Quindío where Amanda, her other daughter, should be, whom they never heard from again. In any case, Elías would have to give her a convincing answer to avoid her anger, so he gently got up from the stool and walked a few steps while searching the majestic peaks of the mountain range, fixing his eyes on several points, raising his left eyebrow.

He pointed, saying, "I'm not absolutely certain, dear. I think that way, at the highest peak, along La Línea, up in the cordillera. I understand that Bogotá is on a high, flat plateau, and that is why it's so cold. But ... enough questions. Let me read this letter quietly, and bring me a glass of red wine to complete my happiness. Yes, dear, that's where it must be." Isabelina accepted the man's answer as the truth. She went into the room, struck a match and lit a candle. Then, making sure to stand facing the direction her husband had indicated, she waved her hands in the air for nine blessings while praying fervently, silently, for each of her grandchildren, for her daughter, and for her son-in-law. Finished, she set the coffee to warm, poured two cups and hurried to sit with Elías, who was pleased with what he had read.

The letters continued coming and going, though with less and less frequency as time went on. It seemed that the routine of the big city reduced the intensity of the affection expressed in the letters. In truth, the two old people were more isolated each day, with a greater chance of facing hardship. The big city, always gray, had hypnotized the people from the coffee plantations, their conformity to city life matching the way the younger ones assimilated the accelerated pace of their teacher's instruction.

Gilberto continued working with Don Octavio Tejada, now his boss, whom he praised for his success as a restaurateur and head of a team of eight street salesmen. Don Octavio was from Medellín; he was a robust man with thick glasses and a graying moustache, who was apparently amassing a fortune while maintaining strict control over his sales staff and others who surrounded him. He was accompanied at all times by his wife, Doña Marina, whose right leg had been amputated at the knee, possibly due to gangrene, but spent her time going from one table to another, smoking away the minutes, leaning on her cane and sometimes propping against the wall her acrylic prosthesis, which everyone thought was real when it was attached. The couple inspired Gilberto's trust, for they had given him a job despite his not having fulfilled his promise of investing in the business. In any case, he had ended up giving them a large part of the little funds he had been able to save during that fateful trip.

Both the restaurant and the warehouse for the merchandise were located in a large house in one of the many traditional working-class neighborhoods in northeast Bogotá. Despite not being in the highbrow northern area, it was frequented by distinguished clients, lovers of good food typical of Antioquia and the other delicacies on the menu. Strolling musicians made a living playing *Los Panchos* favorites in exchange for tips. In the evenings, after nine, the Countrymen's Embassy, as the restaurant was known, became a kind of tavern with overtones of propriety and aristocracy, where dinner was served with eccentric cocktails amid applause for a neighborhood tango show and amateur crooners, topped off at midnight by a musical revue with a star singer.

One of those days, the sun came out more fiercely

than ever in Bogotá. It was so strong that it made Gilberto itch between his shoulder blades, burning through his cloth jacket, the one he wore when working in the street and which bore no resemblance to the elegant ones he had worn in El Marqués. It was a jacket he and María Sucel had agreed that he would only use for work, like a uniform. The cloth was faded by the sun, it had been rained on more than once, and it had the accumulated stench of underarm sweat and muddy water splashed on him purposefully by idiot drivers. Although every week María Sucel washed it with soap and water, and ironed it, the poor jacket looked worn and wrinkled.

One very hot day, Gilberto returned after two in the afternoon to report his sales and put the heavy cart away safely. Seeing that Don Octavio was busy with the accounting with other salesmen, he took the opportunity to settle on a chair for twenty minutes and enjoy a cigarette. He sat in a corner of one of the three rooms in the restaurant, confident there would be nobody inside at that time, as its regular opening time was after four in the afternoon. He leaned back against the wall, balanced on two chair legs, just like he used to do in El Marqués when he sat to read the newspaper.

Suddenly, he noticed he was not alone. Peeking timidly, he saw Doña Marina sitting at a table in the next room, convulsing in front of a group of surprised people he didn't know, who were watching her carefully while remaining very still. He was so surprised that when the woman made a deathly, epileptic grimace, he almost fell off his chair. Fortunately, he didn't swallow his cigarette, his reflexes being like those of a fifteen-year-old avoiding a tumble. Quietly and with great effort he righted himself, but he no longer felt so relaxed. What he had seen had piqued his interest, and he settled in like an eager spectator so as not to miss any of Doña Marina's grimaces, though it was impossible to understand what she was mumbling.

The people surrounding the woman were holding each other's hands and uttering confusing words he couldn't understand. Then they were silent, and Doña Marina began to speak to them in the voice of a child no older than nine. Gilberto, extremely confused by so much cumulative weirdness, linked his fingers together and rested his hands on his belly. He opened his eyes wider and took a deep inhalation of his cigarette, immobile, thinking it wouldn't be right to disturb them with his presence. He remained still and amazed, not unlike a cockroach trapped by a cat and forced to wait for circumstances to indicate how to proceed. Gilberto could never have imagined what his eyes were seeing.

Doña Marina spoke like a child for about five minutes. The attendees looked pleased and respectful. They looked at each other, holding their faces in apparent ecstasy over something that Gilberto couldn't decipher from where he sat. They laughed at something she said. Then everything was silent, until once again Doña Marina began her grotesque contortions, her eyes rolling back in her head. Gilberto thought that she might be having a heart attack, but of course that couldn't be, because it made no sense that nobody was coming to her aid. After five seconds, she curved forward, as if her body were going through a painful mutation, and then, looking beaten, she began speaking in the voice of a cranky old man. The others were startled but did not run off. They looked at one another and listened respectfully. Gilberto was wide-eyed, his ears attuned only to the woman's voice, his heart thumping. He couldn't imagine what strange wonder was happening to his boss's wife, who, with a mottled face and missing leg, held everyone's attention so. He thought that maybe the woman was rehearsing for a play to be performed that same evening in the restaurant, at showtime. Minutes passed, and after one last contortion, Doña Marina once again smiled, her forehead bathed in sweat, looking confused, like someone who has just bumped her head. She took hold of a packet of filtered Marlboros and anxiously lit one. Gilberto felt calmer, seeing her looking as well as she had a few days earlier.

Don Octavio entered the restaurant, seeing that his wife had a meeting there, to ask whether she'd seen Gilberto anywhere. Hearing that, Gilberto showed himself, and before Doña Marina could reply, he interrupted, saying, "Good afternoon, everyone. How are you, Doña Marina? Forgive me, Don Octavio, have you been looking for me? I regret having made you wait. I took a moment to go to the bathroom and got distracted resting my feet." They all greeted him, almost in unison.

Don Octavio stepped away from the group and said, quietly, "No, my man. I just came in. But let's take care of those accounts, for it will soon be time to open, and we haven't even had lunch yet. By the way, would you like to join us for lunch? We're having some delicious tripe and would be pleased if you stayed—well, unless you have something to do at home now."

"That's very kind, Don Octavio. How could I refuse, of course!"

They went into the office, where they reconciled the day's sales and inventoried the merchandise in the cart, resupplying it with some special orders to be delivered the following day to a good customer. Having finished their business, they stepped into the restaurant, where a table was spread with exquisite country delicacies prepared with chopped beef blanket tripe, honeycomb tripe, book tripe, and reed tripe, flavored with pork and potatoes, among other delicious ingredients, surrounded by plantains, avocados, pickles, chopped cilantro and pepper sauce. They enjoyed their fill, amid recollections and pleasant conversation, sharing anecdotes from the past. Gilberto proudly told his life's most important story: the adventure he had trying to win María Sucel's love and make her his wife. The Tejadas, for their part, revealed aspects of their past and present in a bittersweet mix, contrasting Doña Marina's gangrenous leg with their good fortune in improving their lives through their business, helped along, they said, by the forces of good and their infinite faith in God.

The street salesman learned that his employers belonged to a spiritualist congregation, which explained the lady's strange performance. Gilberto was both sated and excited. He learned that when the restaurant was closed, they held séances at a small shrine located at the back of the old house, where any consultation regarding these practices was addressed. According to Don Octavio himself, his wife was a medium and through her gift various spirits were incorporated, such as José Gregorio Hernández and Brother Carlos, a colonel in the Colombian army known for his philanthropy, to whom were attributed healing and other miraculous powers, among other abilities.

One April day, nearing her twenty-ninth birthday, María Sucel was in a community health center waiting room crammed with people in pain. She was hoping that one of the doctors could treat Acasio Elías, her newborn, who she guessed was suffering from colic despite the staranise water that she had been giving him over the past three days in his bottle. Concerned, but infinitely patient, she held the baby and constantly shifted him to ease his discomfort. She noticed a woman near her who was comforting a pale, weeping young woman. After exchanging glances with the patients and some of their caretakers, people in the waiting room began feeling more confident and began chatting about anything, just to dispel the tedium of waiting so long.

Intrigued, María Sucel asked gently, "Ma'am, what ails the young woman? She seems so depressed ..."

Seeming grief-stricken, the woman made sure no impertinent ears were listening and replied, in a murmur, "She had an abortion a week ago, but she's still bleeding."

"Heaven help her! Has the doctor seen her yet?" María Sucel asked with concern.

"Not yet. This is a slow process."

"Is she your daughter?"

"Can you imagine?" the woman replied dejectedly. "She's only fifteen and the boyfriend she's had her whole life got her pregnant, and she was afraid to tell us and chose to have an abortion. She could have died ..."

"Thank God she's alive," said María Sucel. "Have faith that everything will be fine in a few more days. Life puts troubles in our way that affect our spirits, which is where it hurts the most." The woman nodded as she listened. They chatted a while and began the type of friendship that is intensified by being neighbors.

"The girl's name is Lía, and I'm Iphigenia Mendieta," the woman introduced herself. "We're very pleased to meet you. Country people are kind and wise. If only we were that civil here ..." They talked and shared experiences and promised to visit and share daily events.

Lia was called in first, as she had arrived earlier. Almost two hours later, a nurse called for Acasio Elías Cervantes. María Sucel hurried forward. Dismissively, looking everywhere but at María Sucel, the woman held the door open for her and indicated that she should continue along to a room where she was to wait. After twenty minutes, a young doctor came in—a lively, talkative intern who greeted her without showing his face, though she tried hard to meet his eyes. He examined the baby and gave her some explanation regarding the cause for his discomfort and recommending some home remedies and a few changes in eating habits. The doctor explained that sometimes the quality of the breast milk she fed little Acasio could be altered by what she ate.

Calmer now, and driven by need, she timidly took advantage of his good mood to ask about how to avoid pregnancy. The doctor was pleased by the question and very kindly set out to inform her. Approaching a small desk, he removed a trifold pamphlet from a messy pile of papers. He unfolded it and showed her the pictures of several methods, explaining each one and answering all her candid questions. Increasingly convinced that she was leaving behind some of her own deeply embedded ignorance and opening a window of hope, she nevertheless did not dare accept the prescription the doctor recommended for contraceptive pills. Her curiosity proved much stronger than her determination. Merely thinking about having to talk about such a decision with her husband filled her with fear. Gilberto was so wrapped up in the street vending business and buried in his fascination with the Tejadas.

As the weeks passed, Gilberto's time at home grew increasingly scarce, though he never neglected his attention to his children and helped them with their homework. He also tried to fulfill his husbandly duties at night. Although she had begun to adapt his attention to the rhythm method the doctor had explained that day, she had started to handle her sexuality with more enthusiasm, participation, and pleasure. That impulse was a result of her conversation with the doctor and having seen Lia and Doña Iphigenia dealing with the traumatic aftermath of a terminated pregnancy.

Undeniably, the big city confronted the young mother with modern views about her selfless sexual compliance.

She was coming to understand this better since the recent birth of Acasio Elías, which had exhausted her. She was determined not to get pregnant again, but to continue fully enjoying her life with Gilberto.

Fortunately for her, he had been distracted lately, spending long hours reading books by Allan Kardec that his employers had recommended. Written in the mid-19th century, they had a singular way of explaining the manifestation of spirits with observations of these phenomena, and their philosophical consequences. A self-educated man, Gilberto was soon immersed in the principles of natural laws that govern the relation between the visible world and the invisible one. So seductive was the call of spiritism that after two months, his morning newspapers, his naps, and his outings to play billiards with acquaintances at La Granja had been replaced with reading Kardec's extensive spiritual work: *The Spirits' Book; The Book on Mediums; The Gospel According to Spiritism; Heaven and Hell or Divine Justice According to Spiritism; The Genesis, Miracles, and Premonitions According to Spiritism; What Is Spiritism?* and *Spirit Journey.*

María Sucel couldn't ignore the theoretical onslaught of spiritism that Gilberto spoke to her about. He justified each paragraph he would read to her without her even having contested it, wrapped up in philosophical interpretations that made him anxious. She followed along, affectionately and with admiration, understanding that his dedication to something spiritual in no way impinged on her. In any case, he was a good man who showed no perverseness or deviance. She rather enjoyed discussing the emancipation of the soul, sleep and dreams, spirit visits among living persons, the hidden transmission of thoughts, lethargy, catalepsy, apparent death, somnambulism, and even ecstasy, all subjects that encountered spiritist explanations, which her husband proclaimed every time she gave him an opportunity to broach the subject.

After a few weeks, Gilberto announced that he and the Tejadas had decided to venture to the eastern plains to broaden the market with further installment sales of furnishings. According to his employer, it was a virgin market, and the moment was ripe for sowing a client portfolio. The truth was that behind the commercial advantage, they hoped that spiritism would take hold in the plains, following in the steps of Brother Carlos, a mystical character who in turn followed other mediums with roots in Acacias, Cumaral, Puerto López and other mythical towns in the eastern plains near Venezuela.

There was enthusiasm for this plan among the family. After living in the cold lands for a few months, they had found harmony and had learned new tasks and new routines. Gilberto left for the plains full of hopes and renewed strength. María Sucel stayed behind with the children, playing the role of caretaker in a kind of kindergarten where the enrollees were registered for life. Two weeks later, her husband sent her a first remittance with the Tejadas, with money for the family's upkeep and a letter for his wife explaining that he missed her and the children and promising to return the following month, though without specifying a date.

They Wouldn't Serve Them...

...1943

"Waitress! Is there nobody serving customers here? What the hell is going on?" shouted a drunk at around two in the morning, outside a bar in Salamina. The tall man with curly blond hair was neatly dressed; he stood outside the bar complaining, but loath to leave. Over-imbibing had slowed his speech and peppered it with faltering words and inopportune hiccups.

"This is why the Allied diplomats met in Moscow ... they wouldn't serve them more beer," he exclaimed, leaning on a wooden post and pulling a dirty handkerchief from his pocket to wipe the drool from his mouth. "This is why the Allies bombed the Japanese in New Guinea ... because they wouldn't serve them more beer."

He waited a few minutes. Then, lifting his eyes towards the door, where a ray of light filtered through, he continued in a low voice, pointing toward nowhere. "That's why Germany is bombing England ... because they wouldn't serve them beer."

He appeared to be a foreigner, or at least someone from another town, one of the men who often arrived at the bar in the early hours. Late-night visitors, especially those who had drunk too much already, were not welcome, as they typically had no money, talked too much and were generally considered bad news. They arrived complaining about having been charged too much for beer at the place that had just thrown them out. The revelry had been intense and relentless that evening.

"That's why, as of today, the honorable Alfonso López is our president ... because he does drink his beer with all of his ministers!" continued the man, who apparently took an interest in world news, because everything he said made a certain sense despite his drunkenness and ludicrous accent.

"It is my pleasure to sincerely and enthusiastically congratulate your excellency as Colombia's president. The Colombian people's unswerving devotion to democracy is one of the most ... hic," he said, referring to Roosevelt's words to Colombia's then president-elect. "That's why Roosevelt congratulated him ... because he likes his beer too, which he's shared with presidents Olaya and Santos. But they weren't asked to leave the bar, nor were they charged for more beers," he continued indignantly. He then sat down on the curb and, searching through his pockets, pulled out his remaining money. He stood shakily, heading again for the door of the bar. With his right hand, barely able to stay on his feet, he waved one of the barmaids over. She reluctantly asked, "What do you want?"

"A beer ... and a cigarette ... and a match, my lovely late-night lady."

The woman went closer when she saw that he held some money in his hand and asked for it before taking his order. He handed her the money. She counted it, asking, "And you think this is enough for everything you want?"

The drunk did not reply and merely lowered his head while continuing to look at her through bloodshot eyes.

"I'll bring you what this money covers," she declared. "But don't come inside, for they will scold me."

Looking around at the other late-night drunks, he rubbed his chin, scratched his head, and proclaimed again, "That's why Japan will attack Russia ... because the Russians wouldn't send them any beer ... that's why the Japanese have more than a thousand airplanes in Manchuria." He continued to stand there until the woman returned with a glass of beer that she had filled from what remained in other glasses left on tables by dozing drunks. She gave it to him with an unfiltered cigarette she lit herself. Oblivious, the man neither acknowledged the favor she'd done him nor thanked her; nor was he touched. But he picked up his beer and let the cigarette dangle from his mouth. He sat on the stoop of the doorway and gazed out at the rest of the drunks.

"That's why they evacuated fifty thousand children in Milan and will evacuate a hundred thousand more," he muttered to himself. Minutes passed, and the woman began to believe she had the docile drunk under control.

"Well, aren't you the philosopher!" she mocked with a laugh.

"Be calm, little lady. No problem here. That's why the French sunk their own ships ... because the Germans wouldn't sell them beer into the wee hours."

"Well ... what's your deal with Germans, Italians, French? Are you from those parts or what?"

The drunk did not reply; he merely looked at her, sipped his beer and tried to stand up, asking, "May I go inside to piss, or would you rather I do it out here?"

The woman smiled at him and tipped her head, indicating he should follow her. As he entered the bar, tottering, she warned him that he could not stay inside, where other barmaids were serving some drunks who were still awake. Though it was after midnight, the jukebox music went on relentlessly, as did the sound of tinkling bottles and the cigarette smoke that seeped into everyone's clothing, leaving a nauseating stink. The drunk, having finished urinating, returned to the doorway and made himself comfortable there. The barmaid, impressed by his obedience, approached him with another cigarette, which she lit and gave to him.

"You should go home. They're probably waiting for you," she said. The drunk obeyed, but not before making one final statement.

"That's why the military took Gilberto ... because he also liked his beer."

Mockingly, she asked whether he was referring to someone he knew. He did not reply, but gave her an exaggerated wink before heading out to the street and disappearing into the darkness. Nélida, overhearing the drunk's comments to the barmaid, was intrigued to hear him mention a certain Gilberto having been recruited to the army.

Days later, at four in the morning in a location far from that bar, a platoon trotted in formation, exhausted but chanting loudly: "Hey, hey, hey, I am drunk, I eat shit, don't mess with me, I am tired, yessir, yessir ..." These phrases, and others the captain came up with, were repeated by the new arrivals to the battalion every morning at dawn before they went to breakfast and moved on to regular military tasks. Gilberto was one of those soldiers, and his was not a very comfortable situation.

The Brigadier General dreamed of being transferred to the emergency international forces, were the Allied troops to request assistance from López's government for support. It was rumored throughout the fort that this might consist of secret help, for not even the press had been notified. The rumor spread among the soldiers, but nobody knew where it originated. It undoubtedly permeated the minds of those potential patriots.

Gilberto had been at the battalion for two months, and he was no longer a novice. His appearance had changed, and between his shaved head and the uniform, old friends might have found it difficult to recall his usual good looks.

One Sunday afternoon, he lay smoking in his bunk, visualizing the people he cared about. He remembered his mother, Sara, who had been there his whole life, offering support. He missed his acquaintances, his women, his beer, and playing billiards. He missed having someone to talk to about everyday things. He thought about Analdo, his younger brother. The thought of going overseas to fight for someone he didn't know, against people he had nothing to do with, was overwhelming. There was much talk in the army about the war in Europe, and Gilberto was already knowledgeable about the subject. Two months in, he viewed life in the garrison as tedious, though full of daily surprises, most of them involving some sacrifice. He was the only reservist who received no visitors on Sundays, because, having been exiled from his family while roaming from town to town, he had been completely distanced from both his relatives and his billiard pals.

While his mates shared time with loved ones during

visitors' hours, he wrote, with unrefined poetic inspiration, hunched over a small table that separated the bunks. Mostly, he tried to stitch together phrases with some rhyming words, to give sense to his spontaneous thoughts. He wrote out of a desire to express his feelings, to reflect on his good moments, to revitalize his spirit and find some mental harmony. He thought of something that brought him much peace, and wrote a few spontaneous verses evoking María Sucel's little newborn face. While he wrote, his mind was filled with her image, etched into his memory since the day of the baptism. After fingering the folded sheet of paper for a moment, he pulled a box of his belongings from under his bunk and placed the poem carefully inside. Then he proceeded to shine his heavy black boots.

Heavy footsteps approached, dispelling the silence in the bunkhouse. The soldier looked pleased to be the bearer of a summons. "You have a visitor!" he announced.

"Who? Me?" Gilberto asked cautiously, thinking he might be the butt of one of those pranks the older recruits played, knowing nobody would ever come to visit him.

"Who else?" the other man replied cheerfully.

Gilberto wasn't sure about that and didn't want to be the unit's laughingstock. Nevertheless, he replied, "How do I know you guys aren't pulling my leg again?"

"Well, go see for yourself, and be quick about it, because visits don't last all day."

Gilberto decided to do just that and strode ahead to the battalion's visiting room. As he passed through the main entrance, he immediately recognized the loyal Nélida, whose eyes filled with tears upon seeing him, while her lips bloomed with a smile.

The soldier ran toward her, wiping away the tears that

threatened to roll down his cheeks. His voice choked by emotion, he exclaimed, "For heaven's sake, what are you doing here, woman?"

Nélida just peered intently at her friend, who had changed so much.

Gilberto embraced her tightly. "What are you doing here, woman, for heaven's sake?" he repeated.

Nélida was unable to utter a word, so they stood quietly holding each other for a few minutes. They simply breathed, not daring to look at each other. Suddenly, he kissed her neck and set her away from him so he could look her in the eyes. Nélida wiped her nose while she stared at him in disbelief.

"Why didn't you tell me about this?"

"I didn't want anyone to find out. They would worry, and it's not fair to anyone; it's just part of my destiny."

"So, what are friends for, then?" she replied, pretending to punch him in the chest. Feeling calmer, Gilberto kissed her lips, and they sat down to chat affectionately. Only thirty minutes were left in visiting time, and Nélida explained how she had arrived at the battalion, and all the difficulties she'd had in locating him. She also told him how she had learned about his detention in the first place; she mentioned that someone named Elías had asked about him once at the bar a few months earlier, and also that a drunk had said his name in the middle of his ravings. He wondered about Elías's interest but did not consider it important. The other character intrigued him, though, because he couldn't imagine who it could have been and what his relationship might be to him. When the bell rang, indicating that visiting hour was over, most of the recruits hugged and kissed their girlfriends or relatives.

"I'll be back in two weeks," was the last thing Nélida said to him.

"If I'm not here, it'll be because they've sent me off to join the Allies in the fighting," he told her with a certain resignation. She took two packages of cigarettes and some coins from her purse and offered them to Gilberto. He unsuccessfully resisted taking them.

On one February afternoon in 1943, one of the battalion commanders shouted, "Recruit Cervantes!"

"Your orders, Commander," Gilberto replied promptly, smartly clicking his boot heels and saluting.

"At ease, soldier."

"Yes, sir. Thank you, sir." Gilberto relaxed his stance. As if in confidence, the commander approached him and told him to report to the garrison's general office for the District Command Secretary and to ask for Officer Restrepo.

"Immediately, Commander," Gilberto complied. He headed to the office, silently bemoaning his luck.

He assumed, bitterly, that the summons was about his transfer to the war front to serve with the Allies. He crossed himself and silently recited the Lord's Prayer and the Creed. He begged the Virgin Mary to protect him and let him see his mother again, so he could ask her forgiveness. He thought sadly of Nélida. He recalled those childhood games, filled with mischief, on the coffee farm. He thought of Don Acasio, his father, smoking a fat cigar and listening to the radio, spitting into his enameled spittoon. He thought of his sister Romelia and her lovely green eyes. Romelia, who always brought him coffee or an energizing threshed maize drink. And Dora, his older sister, defending him when Doña Sara would punish him. He recalled his adventures with the plantation girls; the kindness of the coffee harvester women; his friends, the mule drivers, who let him come along with their teams that strengthened the area's economy. He thought, and thought, and thought.

When he arrived where he had been summoned, he announced himself as he had been trained to do. "At your orders, Commander!"

"At ease, soldier!" The officer left after indicating that he was to answer a subordinate's questions.

Gilberto didn't move. For a moment, he was infused by panic, his face pale, his lips white. His hands were sweating, and his feet felt frozen. Feeling faint, he rallied his willpower, refusing to reveal his fear, for he knew that doing so was practically a death sentence in the battalion. Not even the commander's aloofness when speaking to him had struck him as strange. He was convinced that this fateful summons was about being transferred to the rumored European war camps. He turned towards the seated corporal and sat down in a chair facing his desk.

The corporal had a small, stout jar of black India ink with which he deftly filled a slender quill. *This idiot was surely chosen as the commander's assistant for his penmanship,* Gilberto thought in the midst of his misery. The privileged clerk took a moment to painstakingly clean the pen's tiny barbs. Then he looked at Gilberto impassively and began to ask questions while writing his answers in a small book.

"Name."

"Gilberto," he replied, clearing his throat.

"First surname?"

"Cervantes."

"Second surname?"

"Cervantes."

The junior officer looked at him sternly and asked again, "Second surname?"

"Cervantes. My parents are first cousins and have the same surname," explained Gilberto.

"Father's name?"

"Acasio Jesús."

"Mother's name?"

"Sara."

"Date of birth?"

"November 3rd, 1921."

The corporal wiped the nib with a small cotton cloth and fed more ink into it, then continued. "Place of birth?"

"Neira."

"Place of residence?"

Gilberto thought about his answer; in the end, faced with his interviewer's expectant look, he chose to reply, "Manizales."

"Address?"

"The Estrada neighborhood."

The man rose from his seat and walked to a wooden file cabinet, from which he removed a file with several partially filled forms. He also opened one of the desk drawers and took out some rubber stamps and a few inkpads, then went to a small side table where there was a machine covered in gray oilcloth; he removed the cover to reveal a lovely black Remington typewriter. Taking his time, he took out the spools of ribbon and adjusted them for reuse, then, picking up the copy he had been filling out by hand, blew on the fresh ink until it was completely dry. Gilberto watched him with outward calm, but internally his apprehension grew. The corporal placed paper into the typewriter roller, justified the margins, and renewed his questions.

"Marital status?"

"Single."

The man turned the roller twice to line up the form with a heading that said Physical Appearance. He looked at Gilberto, and, using only his two index fingers, typed: "Skin color: dark olive. Face shape: oval. Hair: abundant, curly. Hair color: dark brown."

He paused to comment, in poor taste, "Seems like everything about you is dark …" With a mocking smile, he continued typing while reviewing Gilberto's features. "Forehead: flat, high, wide. Eyebrows: arched." Using repeated hits on the "x" key, he eliminated the options for "scarce", "heavy", and "tweezed". For twenty minutes, he continued to observe him and type; to Gilberto, it felt like hours. The man then called him over to a corner of the room, asked for his left hand, pressed Gilberto's index finger into one of the inkpads to coat it with ink, and then took his fingerprint on a square form. The same process was followed to record his left thumbprint and the fingers of his right hand. He asked Gilberto to sit and continued typing on the form, under the heading "Reserve Placement: Mr. Gilberto Cervantes-Cervantes, legal age, is placed in the first line of army reserves, second class, as of January 1, 1942, on his twenty-first birthday, until December 31, 1951, the year of his thirtieth birthday …"

Once he had finished filling out the form, he asked Gilberto to sign it and added several stamps.

The soldier withdrew, and in moments the commander stepped in, saying, "I expect you here, with your belongings, tomorrow morning at ten. Make use of the time until then to say goodbye to your comrades."

"Thank you, Commander," said Gilberto, and as he

was leaving, he took the opportunity to ask, "Commander, might I know what this was all about?"

"You'll know soon enough tomorrow, private," was his superior's terse reply.

Gilberto stood at attention and said clearly while he saluted, "Yes, sir! Permission to exit, sir?"

The commander lifted his hand to his forehead in approval. Gilberto spun on his left foot and left, then headed with concern to where the platoon was trotting. One of the officers in charge called him over to report, then ordered him to fall in and start exercising with the rest of the troops. His comrades tried to ask about the mysterious summons, and Gilberto told them bits and pieces of it, whenever the officer was distracted. By the time they were finished with their exercises, most of the soldiers knew he had to report the following morning at ten. Word spread. He might be the first of the recruits to go off to fight in the war. By sundown, most of them had written letters to family and friends about the possibility of leaving the post for foreign lands.

Resigned, Gilberto packed his belongings and lay down to rest. *Is this the way condemned men prepare for their execution? Is this how they spend their last evening? What a horrible fate this is,* he thought, oblivious to the compassionate looks some other recruits sent his way.

One of them came up to him and grasped his shoulder firmly, saying, "Stay calm, buddy. God knows what He's doing."

Gilberto did not reply, and the barracks were once more silent. He lay back in his bunk, crossed his hands under his head, and continued his contemplation. *If I must die, let it be fighting Hitler ... If I must die, I'll die defending someone.* Sleeplessness prevailed, but thousands of scenarios paraded through his disorderly brain until he finally fell asleep at 3:30 in the morning.

He'd only slept a wink when one of his bunkmates woke him up at 4 a.m. while hurrying to put on his boots, saying, "Get up. They're calling us for a run."

Gilberto got up and dressed quickly in his uniform. *Everything will be harder in the war,* he thought, attempting to cheer himself up. Before going outside, he knelt next to his cot and prayed for a few seconds. Crossing himself, he ran out to catch up to the platoon, whose members were already forming up. After their exercises, the captain gave the order to rest without breaking ranks.

"Reservist Cervantes will be removed today from this battalion!" he exclaimed, with no further explanation. "We must wish him the best of luck in his new life. Dismissed. Go to breakfast!" He looked towards Gilberto and wished him luck, somewhat disdainfully. Gilberto didn't say a word. He watched as his mates walked away and headed to the mess hall, where he only had a cup of watered-down chocolate. After a few sips, he went to shower. Making sure that everything was packed for his departure, he looked at the clock and saw that it was a quarter to ten. Suitcase in hand, he approached his superior to request permission to leave. Arriving at the office, he saw a commander named Arcesio Restrepo giving instructions to several soldiers. He waited, keeping an eye on the clock, considering whether he should interrupt the man if he took too long to acknowledge him. That proved unnecessary, for at two minutes before the hour, the commander looked at him and signaled to him to wait. Once he finished with his instructions, the commander walked to the desk, and, opening the top right-hand drawer, took out a small booklet stamped with the seal of the Republic of Colombia, with several typewritten pages and some notes in India ink.

"Make the best use of this document," he suggested as he approached. "It will help to identify you in case you're ever detained anywhere." Those words made Gilberto feel most unhappy, for they foretold difficult situations. The commander held out his hand, and Gilberto shook it. Then he was shown the door. "Godspeed, private. They're waiting for you outside."

They saluted, as protocol demanded, and Gilberto opened the door leading out of the building.

His mother's face lit up when she saw him. Gilberto just stared stupidly at Doña Sara, not understanding why she was there. He had expected to see a bus loaded with soldiers who would be leaving for the war in Europe, like he was. He looked all around and saw faces that made him jump for joy. The peculiar image of his father smoking a cigar, and each of his sisters. Gilberto couldn't believe that they would allow him to see his loved ones before shipping off to war. Turning, he checked the door he had just exited, to prove that he was indeed outside, and turned again to look at his mother, smiling at him tenderly. Numb with surprise, he shook his head, in denial about everything going on around him. Understanding at last that it was true, he embraced Doña Sara tightly. She stood on her toes to kiss his forehead. Though the others were waiting to greet him, he continued to hold his mother; after a time, he released her and threw himself at his father, who embraced him, holding his cigar between his fingers. Gilberto asked for his blessing, and Don Acasio did so with the same fingers that held the smoking cigar. Then he embraced each of his sisters.

Last came Sigifredo, the youngest, whom he hadn't seen in a very long time, for he had become a cardsharp who was practically never home and spent his time going from one billiard room to another, betting until he hadn't enough left to buy a beer. Gilberto became very emotional, what with all the hugging and jubilation, but in his heart still hovered the ghostly fear of his departure for war. He asked for Doña Sara's blessing, and she blessed him, too, without objections or further admonishment. Seeing her so calm confused him, that she was smiling at such a transcendent moment for him. He didn't understand why his siblings all looked so full of joy. Then he noticed that Analdo was missing and asked about him.

"He's inside with some military people and with a girl. He was the one who brought us here. I didn't even know that you were serving in the army," stated Doña Sara.

A short while later, he saw Analdo leaving the barracks with a smile, in the company of Nélida, Lieutenant Colonel Stricker and Captain Bonet. Cheerful, they all walked towards him. Stunned, he embraced his brother and asked, confused, "What's this, brother? Have you joined the army, or what?"

Analdo guffawed and looked around at everyone, laughing. "Welcome to freedom! Welcome home!" he exclaimed, while Gilberto looked on, not yet understanding Nélida's presence. She had dressed for the occasion like a lady instead of her usual garb. Only Analdo, the army men, and Gilberto knew about her, about her profession, or that Analdo had even become her bedmate, before discovering that he had been that drunk who had been complaining that night because they wouldn't let him into the bar or sell him any beer. As far as the rest of the Cervantes family knew,

Nélida was a respectable woman who was kind to Gilberto and had used her influence to get him released from the army. Gilberto finally understood that all his troubles had come to an end, thanks to his good friend's intervention. She had nobly contacted the family to let them know about his release from the army—at the recommendation of the officers she had finally been able to locate after traveling for many hours to Tolemaida, where they were stationed.

"You definitely owe me for this, and I'll collect payment as I choose," Nélida whispered naughtily in his ear when he came to embrace her. Gilberto smiled, understanding exactly what kind of reward she was claiming. Then, properly solemn, he thanked Lieutenant Colonel Stricker and Captain Bonet for interceding with the brigade authorities in his favor, *for apparent lack of weight*, according to the statement in the military passbook handed to him that same day by Commander Restrepo. They piled into an army truck driven by Captain Bonet, and all went to the Cervantes' house in Neira, where they celebrated until dawn.

Between Bogotá and the Plains

...1968

María Sucel was anxiously waiting for a vital stain to show on her panties, but it wasn't happening. She remembered when, at the age of 13, she had thought she was dying when she had her first period, not knowing what it was. She recalled that ruefully, because now it was the signal she desperately wanted to see. Doña Iphigenia, her dearest neighbor, had come over every day this last week for news about the possible pregnancy.

"Eat this soft-cooked egg mixed with rue," she advised. "It might make you ovulate, Doña María. Maybe the delay doesn't mean a pregnancy," she added affectionately as she gave her the herbal concoction in a small coffee cup and handed her a small spoon.

"From your mouth to God's ear," she replied, resigned. Another day went by, and another, and another, and nothing happened. She went to a health center and had her pregnancy confirmed, and was sad as she walked away. She tucked her straight, silky hair behind a flowered headband, letting it hang over her back and chest. Snuggled into a thick sweater knitted from virgin wool to ward off the morning chill, she walked along aimlessly, becoming more distraught as she thought of her youngest son and how far away Gilberto was. Without giving it much conscious thought, she entered a small coffee shop. Its warm interior was illuminated by sconces on the walls. She sat down at one of only six tables, which was set up for spontaneous games of chess to entertain customers while they drank a cup of coffee and waited for service. The young lady at the counter suggested she sit at a different table and promised to take her order shortly. María Sucel moved quietly and sat with her elbows on the tabletop, pulling her hair in an effort to relieve the heaviness in her mind. A waitress approached from the back of the shop, carrying a sugar bowl and a spoon on an aluminum tray. She placed them on the table and smiled, ready to take her order.

"Good morning, ma'am. What can I get for you today?"

"Something hot, please. Bring me coffee, very hot, boiling, bubbling, so it takes away this coldness in my soul. Really hot, please, because I need to take a long time drinking it while I think about what to do about this new wrinkle in my life." The waitress burst into a laugh. She'd never had anyone order coffee in such an odd way or with such urgency, and she couldn't help but be amused. So did María Sucel, when she realized that something funny had been created from her despair. Now they were both smiling, chuckling about the heartfelt order. The waitress couldn't have imagined the particular details of her customer's life—facing her eighth pregnancy in a row, exhausted after delivering so many babies. She simply took the order, and when she brought the coffee she was quiet, noting that her customer was deep in thought.

María Sucel returned home roughly pinching her belly. One look at her face as she walked through the door told Doña Iphigenia what the results of her errand had been.

In the shadows of her room, she moaned in pain. Thin to the point of being gaunt, she struggled with the discomfort produced by the abortion she'd had at the same place Lía had gone a few days before. She was also struggling with feeling depressed, which came as a shock because she had made her decision independently, without coercion. In the midst of feeling overwhelmed, she thought of Gilberto and was grateful that he wouldn't be back from the plains yet for several weeks. The persistent hemorrhage had stained her sheets, but in her despondent state, she could barely take care of herself properly.

Despite thinking that her struggle with pain was lonely, she had not noticed that a couple of restless eyes searched among the lumps that the gloom let perceive, ready to interpret the origin and cause of the skinny moans. The second of his little ones, Tomas, had woken up because of a tingling in his arm caused by a bad position in his sleep and who when listening to his mother left his eyes wide open while his brothers slept peacefully. After abandoning his state of lethargy, he understood that something was happening and knew immediately that it was his mother.

Afraid of feeling her complaining during so much loneliness and motivated more by love than by an instinct, he sat up and reached her bed without making noise. At that moment María Sucel had already realized that her little Tomas was awake and seeing him arrive weakly, she asked him to lie down again to sleep because when the sun rose, he would go to school. The boy stared at her and in disobedience with his little face framed in a spoiled pout, he replied: "Mom, what do you have? are you sick? do you want me to bring some water?" María Sucel understood that she was exposed and that it might be easy for her to take advantage of her son's naivety to help herself in some way. She asked him not to worry because her discomfort was related to some food that had fallen badly on her but assured him that she would pass it on in the next few minutes. She better suggested that he bring her a sheet of those that were inside the basket of clean clothes, but that he do it without turning on the light because his little brothers could wake up. When he returned, she asked him to extract the wet sheet while she, battered, changed positions to make it easier for the little one to do such a task.

When finished, María Sucel took the sheet, rolled it up and making use of the little energy she had left, and cleaned her body under the blankets. Then, as best she could, turned the sheet into a discreet tie and put it under her bed while her little boy watched, and then asked him to help her arrange the dry sheet again while complaining silently. "Mother, if something went wrong with your stomach, then why are you bloody? Is it that you are going to die?" Tomas asked her and wept fearfully. Maria Sucel pulled him to her chest and hugged him for a moment while in his ear she said in a choppy voice: "You are too small to understand grown up things, but I just want to tell you not to worry. What really happened was that your mommy was going to have another child, your brother, but that little boy preferred not to be born and then he came out of my tummy. That happened this afternoon. I was sad, but thank God I am here well, to love you and your brothers very much for life". The little guy tried to understand, but the subject was confusing. "Tomorrow, you tell me how children are born and how children come out with blood?" The puzzled boy replied. "Yes son", she said hugging him with the strength of her soul and kissed him on his smooth little face. Impressed, Tomas managed to fall asleep, but not before having asked another couple of questions to his mother, who, knowing his presence, hid her suffering so as not to make it more noticeable and awaken new panics in his infant mind.

The new day finally arrived and Maria Sucel in her weakness got up to dispatch her little ones to school. At eight o'clock, Doña Ifigenia arrived to check up on her. After a few days the abortion had begun to be forgotten. María Sucel began to recover her health and in her cheeks the anemic yellowness had begun to say goodbye. Despite her diminished physical condition, María Sucel felt proud for having dared to do what her conscience dictated despite how masochistic and vexatious it might have been. One day, upon his return from school, a sympathetic talk cleared doubts for Tomas, who by dint of circumstances became the little confidant, promising that his father would never find out.

Three weeks later, Gilberto arrived in triumph, loaded with transparent water-filled plastic bags containing a great number of ornamental fish taken from creeks in the eastern plains, which he placed in an aquarium. It was a wonderful gift for his children, whose fascinated eyes were glued to the twists and turns of the fish. For his wife he had brought a pair of chattering parrots from the Macarena jungle, which were, according to some folks from those distant places where he went, a refined species, especially the blue one with a black beak, although the green one was noisier and cuter. Gilberto told them about his adventures on the plains, where he had been able to set up a warehouse of furnishings right in the San Isidro de Villavicencio neighborhood, near the red-light district, and from there he organized sales in all the districts, including the high-toned San José area.

María Sucel enjoyed hearing how he was getting ahead in the new city, and though she wasn't happy about the distance, this also had its benefits for minimizing his lovemaking and avoiding future pregnancies. With time, she was growing more confident with that rhythm business and wanted to begin taking birth control pills, as her doctor had recommended. Gilberto's sojourns in Bogotá were increasingly shorter, and María Sucel's weekend trips to the plains had gotten to the point of being routine.

"Mark my words, Don Octavio, those bandits will continue with their old tricks on the plain. That's because one of the ones captured was a so-called ... Umar Alreju, apparently the leader of the group, and he had been granted amnesty by Rojas Pinilla's government, even though he had been found guilty of genocide and other crimes in the past. That's unforgivable in this country ... on one hand, the Communists and hooligans, on the other the idiots and slugs. That business about forgiving and forgetting is more foolishness from the generals and those shameless politicians," stated Gilberto, wrapping up a heated political discussion with his boss. Don Octavio chewed on the temple of his eyeglasses as he listened attentively, reaching supernatural conclusions through a mind that, in its alienation from reality produced by reading Kardec, soon formulated a prophetic sermon. He affirmed, dispassionately, that the spirits of those pesky outlaws had certainly been people who had caused much damage to humanity in their past lives, and it wouldn't be surprising if, in other incarnations, one of them had been that bloodthirsty Pablo Morillo himself.

"Do you remember him from history class?" he asked Gilberto. "The one they called *El Pacificador*, who silenced anyone who rejected Spain's presence in what they called the New Kingdom, silenced them with bullets and swords. Maybe one of them was one of those Spanish conquistadors who exterminated our Chibcha or our Quimbayas, or the Incas or the Aztecs. Or one of those soldiers who did away with those Navajos up north, and have now come to this world reincarnated as guerrilla fighters to continue paying for their crimes. It's possible that their souls have been purified by their death; since they were young, they had to return to the supernatural world and will continue to wander, waiting for the chance to return to the terrestrial plane for complete purification." Gilberto listened to him closely.

"We should pray for them," suggested Don Octavio. Gilberto agreed and added that maybe Doña Marina could invoke the spirit of one of those outlaws, since, based on what they heard on the radio, it would be easier to know what the future held for the country by asking those traveling souls than by listening to the news.

"We will never know for certain what it is those people who seek to be killed are truly after," said Gilberto. Don Octavio smiled, scoffing that one must not use the spirits to learn about current issues. He then added that it could be dangerous for a medium to invoke a tormented soul, and that Doña Marina could remain in a trance, because those spirits are very rebellious and would make her suffer greatly, and it would be best to leave those souls alone. He also affirmed that some benevolent spirit would surely give them all the information.

"By the way, Don Octavio, things are not going well in the United States, with that black man getting assassinated …"

"Yes, indeed … they killed Martin Luther King. How sad; it was the death that awaited that soul. Maybe yesterday it ended its purification. Say, Don Gilberto, changing the subject, how is your family?"

"Fine, fine, thank you for asking. The children study sensibly, and the younger ones tirelessly play all day long. My wife is a bit anxious about having a house of her own. It was something I had promised when we left Armenia, and I haven't even started to look for one yet. I just hope that you could tell me, when do you think you'll be able to pay back the money I lent you?" A shadow crossed Don Octavio's face. He wished he hadn't asked about the family, and, uncomfortable, he raised his arms to stretch his back, as he thought about how to respond.

His reply was quick and accompanied by an unconvincing, fake smile. "We'll have your money ready next month. Let's hope that the business in the plain improves, because things have slowed down at the restaurant. These days, there's not too much to go around. I'll let you know when we have it." He went to his employee and gripped his shoulder, leaving him puzzled. "You're a good talker, Gilberto, but it's gotten late. We have much yet to do."

One night in May, the children were asleep, but María Sucel wouldn't be going to bed yet for another hour or two. She would wait for her husband to finish reading Kardec, after having blessed a pitcher of water into which he had stirred alcohol-based lotions to be used as a body ointment, or better, as a curative medicine for high fever or against bodily or spiritual assaults. In those days, Gilberto was deep into the study of medicinal herbs and prayers, and everyone in the family had become accustomed to humoring him.

María Sucel used the time to darn a bunch of worn-out socks, with holes right in the seam near the big toe. Thanks to her experience after many years of embroidery, she always mended them perfectly so that Gilberto could avoid having to buy new socks. Although he was concentrating on his reading, with his glasses perched halfway down his nose, he occasionally looked over the rims at his wife, who every once in a while got up to reheat another cup of coffee in the kitchen, usually coinciding with Gilberto lighting up another cigarette.

"Honey, I hope all this reading won't take away from the time we have to be together. Tell me how the family is doing in my absence, and whether you've missed me, at least a little?"

"You know very well that I will always miss you. We've been together many years, haven't we?"

"We have, but it saddens me that I've had to leave you alone so much. Coming to this city has meant sacrifices I had never imagined."

"The only thing I miss with all these changes is that, even though the most beautiful flowers in the world come from this place and are sent all over the planet, there are never any arriving at my house. Maybe I have to write another acrostic? I'm not fifteen anymore!" After having been pleased to hear his sincerity, she reproached him, and he was ashamed.

"Don't say that. That makes me so sad. I've been really careless!" replied Gilberto. "Don't think I love you any less because I don't send flowers. Things have changed, and I don't have Mrs. Ectilvia's flower shop nearby anymore. She was always punctual about making sure I had fresh flowers for you. I'm so ashamed of myself! I know that's not a good answer. I don't have any excuse," Gilberto declared, and kissed her, hiding his embarrassment.

"Don't take it to so much to heart," his wife said, "I was only teasing."

Once the lights were out, they blended with the night. After so many years, they knew how to make love quietly. Maybe they even enjoyed it more that way, with their passion wrapped in silence. They kissed, and their caresses released their feeling of belonging to one other. They'd enjoy each other until their passionate urges quieted and they found tenderness. Often, when they had finished, they shared an almost silent conversation, where he told her of his exploits in the plains, and she told him of the children's achievements in school and at home. She never said a word about the abortion, or about the birth control pills, but she did speak about her new friend, Doña Iphigenia. She talked about her without mentioning the daughter's abortion, either. He, in turn, didn't speak about Don Octavio's intemperate reply when he'd asked about the money owed to them. But she did comment on the promise of a house that would be bought when the few funds left from Armenia were used for the down payment. The chat ended with his evading the issue. In the end, she slept warmly after weeks of loneliness.

Though Gilberto thought and thought about it, he couldn't pinpoint the reasons for the strength of the following he had garnered through his preaching and practice. He didn't claim to have miraculous powers, or even boast about being a medium or anything along those lines, but he seemed to have a charisma, bolstered by confidence, that kept him well surrounded by ladies. His good heart made him an ideal and handy advisor, especially for the unfortunate people in the Eastern Plains, and in Bogotá as well, where he already had a considerable circle of clients.

Many people came looking for Brother Gilberto, which provoked feelings of admiration and amazement in María Sucel. She had never imagined him becoming someone who practiced a discipline different from everything Isabelina had drummed into her during her whole life. Her amazement grew as she noticed images of Jesus Christ being mixed with books on medicinal plants and the writings of Allan Kardec, together with numerous bottles of lotions, salt, and water blessed by himself, all packed into jars of various sizes that he gave away freely, jars the devotees returned to him with fervent thanks and occasional voluntary gratuities that he accepted awkwardly.

The trips to the plains continued; María Sucel visited him often, taking the opportunity to spend time with some of her young ones and bring home some money.

The Acrostic

...1956

Gilberto was having a meal with his mother, who was anxious to know how they would make a living in Armenia, where they had moved to get away from the cold in Neira. He told her that he had visited about fifteen places looking for work before he found a dry grocer whose owner, a Don Juvenal Betancourt, had interviewed him and agreed that he could start the following day. After only a few days, he had already gained the boss's trust to such a degree that he was placed in the position of manager at El Marqués, with several workers under his supervision, such as porters, watchmen, and an assistant to help with the daily bookkeeping, tracking orders, and keeping inventory. He was also in charge of a couple of brown cats whose job it was to keep an army of mice under control and away from the grains they would otherwise avidly gnaw on. El Marqués was undoubtedly the most famous warehouse in the city, the one that supplied most of the local stores and small businesses in the outlying areas and in other towns. Gilberto also coordinated home deliveries for their clients, a task carried out by youngsters who worked independently, using carts they built themselves to carry the heavy sacks in exchange for tips.

El Marqués was located in something called La Galería, a large, one-story building with storefronts on all four sides, facing both the outside and the interior of the building. La Galería filled what had become the most popular block in the city, even more popular than the cathedral. Villagers and neighbors, from all walks of life, came there in search of bars, brothels, shoe stores, coffee shops, restaurants, bakeries, and even a barbershop where men flocked for haircuts and to have their beards or mustaches trimmed. Facing one of its corners was the majestic, imposing church of San Francisco, with its hundreds of pigeons and dozens of Franciscan priests. The priests wore distinctive Carmelite robes with white cords at their waists and heavy sandals on their feet. The place was inevitably packed with scores of beggars; after panhandling the churchgoers as they exited the church, the beggars would seek food handouts or attempt to sell trinkets to earn their living.

Still a favorite bachelor among the young ladies who came to the warehouse with their parents, Gilberto had become restrained and elusive, unlike during his youth. The only relationship he still slightly maintained was with Nélida, who lived in Manizales with the three children she'd borne from her anonymous clients, one of which was presumably his. Although Nélida never demanded anything for the boy, since she lived with a man who took care of her and her offspring, her old friend provided a small allowance for the boy's expenses.

Lieutenant General Gustavo Rojas Pinilla's rise to power on June 13, 1953, with the unconditional support of presidents Ospina Pérez and Urdaneta Arbeláez, marked a new reality at every level across the country, a situation evident in La Galería, whose harmony was about to be affected by the military government's restrictions on barrooms and taverns. Newspapers promised to print special editions with the latest news.

That day, Gilberto had gone out to buy a bag of buns to take to Doña Sara, and he approached a street vendor who was serving a slender woman wearing a large scarf over her head. The woman paid for her purchase and prepared to leave, not having noticed that he was watching her with great interest. Wanting her to notice him, wanting to speak to her, he nevertheless kept still, realizing that the lady might feel uncomfortable at being approached with impertinent questions. He settled for merely watching her as she walked away.

"How many buns would you like, sir?" the vendor asked as he clacked the metal tongs that he used to take up the buns and fill the customers' bags.

"Twelve, please. Are they nice and fresh?" asked Gilberto, his attention fully on the lady that had just left.

"Delivered just this afternoon," the bakery seller replied. Gilberto paid, took the bag and the change and, still curious, asked the man if he knew the woman he had just served. The vendor told him she was a regular client who bought buns every day after mass at San Francisco church. Gilberto asked her name, but the man didn't know; trying to be helpful, he added that today had been an exception, and that the lady usually came by earlier, as she surely would do the following day. Gilberto thanked him and walked to his house in the Granada neighborhood, about fifteen blocks away. Alone with his thoughts, he endeavored to remember any detail that might help him identify the intriguing woman.

The following morning, when he unlocked the heavy padlocks on the metal curtains protecting El Marqués, the bun seller's clacking tongs reminded him of the woman. He called to the vendor, and after buying something, he asked again about the woman. The man assured him that at that very moment she was surely at church.

Gilberto left some instructions for his employees and went back out, saying he was going for coffee. He walked to the church and crossed himself on entering. His gray eyes focused on the kneeling women at prayer. The mass was over, but there were still people in the confessionals owning up to their sins and cleansing their souls of remorse. He walked slowly to avoid disturbing those who prayed, made offerings, or just dozed near the saints of the stations or at St. Francis's feet. He walked past several women but couldn't find her among them. He had decided to return to the warehouse when, standing at the top of the church stairs, he saw the bun seller hand the woman a bag. He ran down the steps without taking his eyes from her in the crowd and walked quickly to catch up with her. She strolled with her head down, unmindful of those around her, lost in thought. A black shawl was arranged over her head, covering abundant, straight hair. Gilberto walked by her and felt a kind of *dèja vu*. In his mind, he saw a younger version of this woman's face, someone he had exchanged a few words with one day towards the end of the '30s. Quickening his pace, he passed her and, after a few feet, turned around, pretending to have forgotten something, and walked back, intending to memorize her features. The woman, who was rearranging the buns she had just bought, could not help looking at him.

They stared at each other, speechless, both reminded that they were old acquaintances whose initial meeting had left them with a multitude of garbled feelings. It was Isabelina, Elías's wife, now fifteen years older, yet still beautiful and slender. Somewhat rattled by this unexpected meeting, she rearranged her scarf while her mind went back to the past. She remembered the face of a young man being taken into the army back in 1942, along the road to Manizales. Looking at him carefully, she verified that those gray eyes she had once seen filled with sadness now shone happily to see her. Many years had passed since then, and she couldn't be sure of his true identity.

She was the first to speak, breathtakingly serious, looking at him with profound interest. "You look familiar to me …"

"Yes, dear lady. You also remind me of someone with whom I shared important moments," exclaimed Gilberto, moved by his memories yet speaking with his customary chivalry.

"Do I? And what moments would those be? I wonder if they are the same ones I recall," she replied, sure she was looking into the same gray eyes that had made her so sad at María Sucel's baptism, fifteen years ago now.

"Do you remember when María Sucel spit her pacifier to the floor and I helped you to pick it up?"

"I remember it well, as if it was yesterday," Isabelina said, emotion flooding her as this brought to mind happy memories of that unforgettable time in the church at Salamina.

"Do you also remember, ma'am, that you saw when the soldiers hit me on the road near Manizales about eleven years ago?"

Isabelina briefly relived the despair she'd felt at the time, feeling pleased that, after so many years, the somber young man she had seen was well. She extended a motherly hand and laid it against his face. Then she let it slide to his shoulder, and finally she took both his hands, and told him in a few, heartfelt sentences how she had hurried to her prayers that day, feeling so moved with compassion for his pain. She also told him she had spoken to two officers in an attempt to learn where they had taken him, and finally, shared with him that Elías himself had visited various bars in Salamina, searching for information as to his whereabouts. Touched, Gilberto listened to what she said; he had never imagined how much the Barojas had cared for him after only a few brief encounters.

"God bless you, ma'am. Seeing you makes me indescribably happy. It reminds me of what I felt the day María Sucel was baptized." Isabelina, wrinkling her brow, was surprised at how clearly he had remembered her daughter's name, and, smiling timidly, told him so. Gilberto pulled his wallet from his pocket and carefully took out a small piece of paper, its folded edges worn over the years. He opened it very carefully and let her see the name *María Sucel* noted there, next to the baptismal date.

"I will always remember the feeling of peace her inquiring little eyes and her tender babbling inspired in me," he tenderly explained.

"You surprise me, Don Gilberto," was all she could think of to say. Taking the piece of paper, she stared at it for several seconds and then looked steadily at Gilberto as she returned it to him. "I am very pleased to see you, Don Gilberto, you are looking quite well."

"Thank you, ma'am—" Isabelina interrupted him,

delicately stressing her name. She told him that Elías was well, except that he had a persistent cough. She said that María Sucel was all grown up and at fifteen had become the prettiest young lady in the neighborhood.

"I work here in La Galería, at the El Marqués warehouse, where you can always find me if you ever need me. You should stop by one day with Don Elías. I would very much like to have a coffee with you."

Some days later, while Gilberto was arranging merchandise on the shelves, he heard someone coughing behind him. Gilberto turned around and found himself staring at Elías Baroja, whom he easily recognized. He was sorry to see Don Elías looking so haggard as the man pulled out a handkerchief and wiped his mouth and graying mustache. He realized Don Elías's presence there was a direct consequence of his running into Isabelina. He walked over and greeted him warmly.

"How are you, young man?" asked Elías. "I thought they had killed you in the army. You never came back, and I looked everywhere for you, thinking to offer you a job in the road construction camp."

Gilberto smiled and gave him a warm hug.

"I am very happy to have found you again," Elías continued, trying to conceal the discomfort caused by his cough. "You are looking very well. How long have you been in Armenia?"

"Just two years, but I'm already a fan of Quindío Athletic Club. Would you care for something to drink, Don Elías? Or better, let's go across the street and have a coffee, and talk." They left the building and crossed the street. They had several coffees as they sat and chatted for almost two hours. And so Gilberto renewed his friendship with Elías, to whom the years had not been kind.

Elías opened the door in response to the insistent knocking of eager knuckles. Pleased to see each other again, they shook hands energetically. The older man stood to one side, leaving room for his esteemed visitor to enter.

"I came by to say hello and drop this off," said Gilberto as he set down a heavy sack full of groceries, a gift for Elías. They sat in the parlor with half a bottle of spirits and some glasses.

"I hope my visit is not inopportune, Don Elías." Elías waved off the comment with his hand and began to talk about current events. The young man offered a spontaneous toast, and his host did the same. They were soon wrapped up in an animated conversation, talking about the seven hundred guerrillas who had surrendered their weapons in the eastern plains, and reflecting on the number of people who had turned to crime. They lauded General Rojas Pinilla for disarming the insurgents. Then the conversation moved on to the war in Korea and the return of Colombian soldiers who had been imprisoned. They spoke proudly of President Eisenhower's congratulations to the Colombian government, words which surely, they agreed, had accounted for the rise in coffee prices in international markets.

"The country is undoubtedly more peaceful under Rojas," suggested Elías.

"Well, who isn't more peaceful with a military government?" wondered Gilberto, as his attention was drawn to a wooden needlework hoop left on the sofa, which tautly held some fine linen delicately embroidered with colorful silk threads. Noting his interest, Elías explained that the cloth was a pillowcase or bedsheet that María Sucel was finishing to present at the school where she studied. It occurred to Gilberto to ask whether she could embroider something as pretty for his mother Sara, for her birthday. Elías's eyebrows shot up and he spread his hands, indicating that he wasn't really sure.

When the bottle was empty, the guest bid his host farewell, and the older man accompanied him to the door and watched as he walked away. He then went back into the house, leaving the door and windows open, as was the custom in that peaceful land.

For the first time, María Sucel faced the challenge of embroidering something for someone else, after her father told her about the young man who had visited. Excited, she opened the door of a heavy wooden cabinet and removed a round box adorned with flowers in pastel colors, in which she kept her sewing things. She put them in order, took the frame with the weaving and brought it to her chest dreamily and kissed it. She and Isabelina spent some time defining the details of the project.

"Today is certainly a day to celebrate!" exclaimed Elías on the day he delivered the embroidery. Puffed up with pride as he stood in the middle of El Marqués, he assured Gilberto that he had in his hands a veritable work of art made by his daughter's hands. The young manager caught Elías's enthusiasm and called each of his helpers to join them, until a considerable group of people had gathered, including clients. He started to open the package, but realized that he was much too clumsy and might damage it. He called on the only woman in the warehouse to help him handle the items without ruining them.

"Ophir! Please come here," he shouted, searching around the store. Almost immediately a graceful brunette approached, about twenty-five years old, and helped him while praising the beautiful handiwork.

It was four-thirty in the morning. A cold wind filtered through the cracks in the doors, while Isabelina's shadow bounced off the kitchen walls. The aroma of fresh coffee challenged Elías's sleep; he had been waking up to the smell of coffee for many years now. Isabelina's day started early, though preparing breakfast for the camp had been replaced by a kind of morning routine that began with her walk to San Francisco church, where she attended five o'clock mass and often also the six o'clock mass, for she had so many prayers to offer for those who had asked it of her. But this Tuesday was a special day. Gilberto had accepted an invitation to share a meal of stewed beans with the Baroja family, and that meant a busy day for Isabelina and the girls. Before heading to church, Isabelina poured a cup of coffee and took it to the bedside table near her husband, who was already smoking a cigarette in the dark.

"Don't delay, dear, today we have company!" exclaimed Elías as he coughed.

Isabelina went to the kitchen, poured another cup of coffee and hurried to leave it for María Sucel. She left it on the bedside table, where she placed a glass of fresh water every night. A few minutes later, she mingled with the other ladies who were also walking to church. Her daughter, now awake, got up and put on her robe, went to the bathroom and rinsed her mouth out with water. Then she pulled back her hair with a band she had wrapped around her wrist. It was a special day for her, for after hearing about Gilberto and preparing the embroidery for his mother, that Tuesday she would have the chance to meet him in person.

She took care of getting everything ready and finished

her tasks by placing a vase of fresh tuberoses on the table, which showed off to great advantage the embroidered cloth she had decided to put out to please this man, who would no longer be a stranger after today. Elías was still out, buying more *aguardiente* and some beer, in case that was their visitor's preference.

Isabelina combed her straight hair in front of the mirror at her dressing table and, taking a tortoiseshell hair stick, wrapped it into a subtle bun. She wore a black dress, with a pleated skirt and a wide woven belt. Her husband dressed just as carefully, in a dark jacket, an elegant felt hat with a black band, and a French-cuff shirt with onyx and gold cufflinks. María Sucel curled her hair into tight loops that bounced prettily when she walked and made her look younger. She had dressed in white, in a lacy blouse with puffed sleeves and a very wide skirt that reached almost to her ankles and showed off her tiny waist. Her fresh and slender figure was clearly feminine, and with her lovely smile, she presented a harmonious image of a promising fifteen-year-old. Elías kept watch at the window so that Gilberto would not catch them unaware, and Isabelina also peeked out occasionally.

"He's coming, he's coming!" he announced, and the women scrambled to be ready to greet their guest, to whom the host waved from the window as if he had just now noticed him. "Hello, there, friend, come along, I'll open the door."

Gilberto smiled and stood outside the door, and when it opened, he walked in and cheerfully handed Isabelina a bouquet of flowers. He then turned towards young María Sucel and bowed, extending his right hand towards her.

"You're María Sucel, aren't you?" he asked, seeing

her standing next to her mother. María Sucel looked at him shyly and nodded. "Well, I am very pleased to meet you. I haven't seen you in fifteen years." Everyone, even María Sucel, laughed at his joke, understanding exactly to what he was referring. They thought Gilberto was very personable, and his comment helped everyone feel less formal.

"Your embroidery has made quite a sensation; some people have even asked me whether I had it brought from Europe. My mother will be so pleased with me, thanks to you. Tell me, miss, where did you learn such a lovely skill?" The girl could not hide her shyness and, blushing, looked at Elías for support. He explained that the nuns had taught her, but that her mother had provided the best ideas.

They shared some appetizers they had prepared for the occasion. Gilberto and María Sucel were alone for the first time while Elías went to prepare drinks. She sat facing him, but didn't dare say a word, she was in such awe. Very sure of himself, their guest started the conversation by telling her that her name had accompanied him for the last fifteen years. He said, respectfully, that he'd like her to know that her eyes shined as brightly as they had on the day of her baptism. He confessed that carrying the image of her bubbly face in his mind had helped him through his most despairing times.

"Your words sound like they are a part of something that only you are aware of," was the only thing María Sucel could think of to say. Her youth and freshness held a strange fascination for Gilberto. Trying not to let his interest show, he attempted to memorize her figure and her face; no detail escaped him, and he took rigorous advantage of every opportunity to observe her from her head to her toes. As for María Sucel, she observed him curiously, trying not to reveal how intensely intimidated she was. She did try, however, to note the tall young man's gray eyes, which were so very uncommon around those parts. She considered him a handsome, charismatic person who exhibited such friendliness it inspired everyone to treat him courteously.

Seeing her father coming, she stood to leave and remove herself from the responsibility of conversation. After a few minutes the girl returned to the parlor, carrying a crystal vase in which she had arranged the bouquet of flowers Gilberto had brought, carefully distributing them nicely and placing the vase on the wooden table, next to the tuberoses she had previously placed there. Gilberto watched her covertly, not missing a single detail. When she finished arranging the flowers, she looked at him and, trying not to interrupt the conversation, asked if he liked it. He nodded and gave her a big smile; María Sucel went back to the kitchen, where Isabelina was waiting for her with several trays of food ready to carry to the table.

"Would you gentlemen like to go into the dining room now, or rather wait until later?" María Sucel asked them when she returned.

"I think we're ready to eat," their guest replied. "It smells very good, and I swear to you that I've not eaten much today, in order to fully enjoy this wonderful meal that you've prepared." The table was ready, and at each setting there were Antioch-style beans with rice, fried pork rinds, roasted beef, slices of ripe plantain, and sausage. Next to each plate of culinary delight, there was a cup of maize grits with milk and shaved raw sugar. The meal could not have been tastier, and it extended for a couple of hours. The four of them shared stories, as they told the young woman all the anecdotes that had brought them together in the past.

She realized that he had many reasons to be grateful to her parents, and even guessed that he was proud of his own story.

Over time, the relationship between the Baroja Sánchez family and Gilberto grew until it formed a certain dependency. The young manager acquired the habit of having the weekly shopping delivered to their home, and Isabelina would stop by to greet him occasionally after mass, taking the opportunity to pay him for the supplies. He always included in the delivery a bunch of fresh flowers, but he was unaware that it was María Sucel who usually arranged them in vases, never feeling that Gilberto sent the flowers because it was his custom and to be nice. Isabelina, however, knew that Gilberto sent them to be polite, since he had arrived with flowers on that first visit to their home. The mother considered it a charming gesture, which she returned by taking him small cakes that she made herself. Elías also stopped by to chat at least once a week, and every two weeks they went together to the barber to get their hair trimmed.

Arriving from school, and motivated by curiosity, María Sucel walked into the kitchen and wondered that there had been no flowers delivered that Monday. Before asking about it, she noticed that there were no flowers in any corner. Though she thought it strange, she understood that Gilberto had no obligation to send them, but the hours passed, and the missing flowers filled her with sadness, though she didn't know why. *How sad the vase looks without fresh flowers,* she thought. *How sad the corner looks without the vase filled with flowers.* She walked around the parlor, went to the window and leaned her elbows on the sill, looking out to the vastness of the street that disappeared in a straight line towards the center of the city. Again, she thought, *How sad our house looks without the vase full of flowers. How sad I feel without flowers.* She remained there for a few moments, and then went out on the patio, where Isabelina was at the cement sink, washing clothes. María Sucel offered to help with the washing in order to keep her mind busy.

Days passed, and still no flowers arrived. María Sucel tried to find some way to know the reason, but her excessive discretion played against her purposes, and she preferred not to ask any questions directly. She then had the idea of asking her mother to let her make up the shopping list, and this is what she did:

>   **F***lour*
>   **L***entils*
>   **O***lives*
>   **W***hite vinegar*
>   **E***ggs*
>   **R***olled oats*
>   **S***alt*
>   **F***laked coconut*
>   **O***regano*
>   **R***aisins*
>   **M***aize, ground*
>   **A***pple cider*
>   **R***ice*
>   **I***ncense sticks*
>   **A***lcohol*
>   **S***ix bags of beans*
>   **U***nflavored gelatin*
>   **C***ans of sardines*
>   **E***ggs*
>   **L***inseed oil*

It was the first time there were products on the list that were not sold by El Marqués. Confused, the manager packed up what he had available, and the rest he obtained from colleagues in the building. When the task was finished, Gilberto verified the list and the prices, adding it up by hand on a tablet printed with the company's name. He took a few moments to correct and make sure everything was in order. He picked up the list from the countertop to tape it to the bag where the items were packed, and looked at it one last time. That's when he noticed that the first letter of each word on the list seemed to be darker, and in capitals, which made them more noticeable.

Gilberto was incredulous when he realized that the most subliminal message lay right before his eyes, filling him with joy. An eloquent phrase appeared when he joined each capital letter of the first twenty items on the list: *Flowers for María Sucel,* he read. Now he understood why there was incense on the list, since there were no dry goods starting with the letter "i". The same with the raisins, and alcohol, and even olives, linseed oil, and eggs. He realized that María Sucel was asking for something, and he recalled that the week before, he hadn't been able to send flowers along with the delivery because the flower vendor had been ill. He thought of her affectionately, but was concerned about the way she had hidden her request and had run the risk of it being discovered. She was daring, but smart and sweet.

From that day forward, he kept the girl's message in his wallet like a treasure. He folded it and placed it next to the pale note written in 1939 with the name María Sucel, and the short poem he had written in the army in the early '40s.

He was pleased with his discovery of the message but had mixed feelings; when he thought of Elías and Isabelina's kindness, he was secretly wrapped in a feeling of sadness. He didn't dare think of the fifteen-year-old with anything but a feeling of friendship, despite her provocative request for flowers. It was improper to think of her as a woman. So he decided to have the order delivered without focusing on the feelings the young woman awoke in him. He guessed that revealing he had understood the message would end up miring him in a compromising situation. He bought a bouquet of tuberoses and sent them with a note explaining the flower vendor's illness, to avoid the complications of acknowledging he'd seen the acrostic.

Thus it was unclear to María Sucel whether the flowers had arrived because of her secret message, or whether, perhaps, it hadn't even been discovered. It occurred to her that maybe someone else had found and deduced the acrostic, and she was embarrassed. In any case, she breathed in and enjoyed the fragrance of the flowers tremendously as she arranged them in the corner, in their usual vase with water. Pulling off a petal, she took it to her room and placed it inside a notebook, where between each set of pages, as though in a herbarium, she kept a petal from each bouquet that had been received from El Marqués. Below each petal, she had written the date when it arrived. Only the page for the previous week was empty, though she had written there the date and a question mark.

Flowers

...*1957*

Isabelina knelt as she waited for the service to begin, her head covered with a black shawl, and carefully perused the devotional booklet corresponding to that Wednesday in April 1955. The church was almost empty; only a few of the faithful were present, quietly whispering their prayers. An acolyte painstakingly prepared the altar for the following service, placing an altar cloth impeccably to cover the front supports, then adjusting the microphone next to the missal. He raised it to the level of his mouth, possibly to ensure it was at the proper height for whoever would read parts of the homily.

This day was different from other days, because the government of Rojas Pinilla had ordered the press in Armenia to be censored, impeding many editorials from being published. Nevertheless, the citizens had learned about important news from around the world, such as the death of Albert Einstein.

Isabelina left the church half an hour after mass, having prayed several additional novenas. As usual, she stopped to buy some buns from Don Aniceto. Then she went to El

Marqués to greet Gilberto and discreetly asked to speak to him. He gave his employees instructions and asked the lady to accompany him to one of the coffee shops in the building, where they ordered only coffee. Isabelina's attitude made him slightly apprehensive, even more so when he saw her carefully digging through her patent leather purse, then taking out a rose petal with a heart pierced through it. Gilberto was embarrassed, and he felt his face growing hot immediately, revealing how perturbed he was.

"Can you explain to me the true reason for the deliveries of flowers to our home?"

He paled; the Barojas had never questioned him about anything. He searched his brain for an adequate reply, and finally told her it was something that he was pleased to do; that he did the same for his own family. Implacably, Isabelina asked whether those flowers also had hearts drawn on their petals. Gilberto lowered his eyes, not able to look at her. Isabelina took from her purse the notebook where María Sucel had organized her herbarium, and showed him each of the pages with the evocative petals, silently recriminating him for every single one of them.

"Only an older man like you would dare to court a young girl. You could be her father!" she exclaimed angrily. He looked at her meekly, then took out his wallet and, one by one, laid on the table the pieces of paper he had been keeping forever. She watched him worriedly. She knew about the worn sheet with her daughter's name from the baptism, but hadn't ever seen the poem from 1943, nor the market list with its hidden acrostic.

"Fate has been circumstantially bringing us together," he said respectfully as he showed her the shopping list.

She listened to him and read the acrostic, and couldn't

avoid tears. Her accusation had led to an anguished confession that made her think about every possible connotation. Perplexed, she wiped her cheeks and looked at him bitterly. She was more confused now than when she had left the house, full of anger. Her regard for this friend had changed course, and her feelings foretold an imminent estrangement. She couldn't help but notice the sadness that came over Gilberto's eyes, just as on the day of María Sucel's baptism, or when she had seen him being transported for induction into military service. He waited quietly, his head bowed, to be scolded for his apparent disloyalty, but Isabelina merely looked at him with annoyance, trying to find relief from her troubled thoughts. Gilberto didn't dare to look at her. He toyed with the notebook while quietly looking through it. Isabelina gently withdrew it and put it back in her purse; she stood, wiped her tears for the last time, and left. He watched the gentle breeze coming through the door ruffle the three pieces of paper on the table. They were testament to a story that had developed over eighteen years.

A very distressed María Sucel searched in her closet for her treasured notebook with the messenger petals, which she hadn't seen since the previous day. Distraught, she looked in every nook and cranny, under the bed, on shelves, in the parlor. Her eyes lit on every object she could think of. Back in her room, she flopped on the bed and stared at the ceiling for a few minutes, angry that someone might know her secret. Suspecting that her collection had already been discovered, she still continued to look for it. Thinking that maybe her youngest sister had taken it, she urged her to help finding it, with no luck.

Hours passed, and the notebook was still missing.

Isabelina returned, and everything appeared to be normal. Mother and daughter greeted each other affectionately, both internally full of despair, which they hid to avoid questions. When the girl went out to see her best friends, Isabelina took the opportunity to place the notebook under some shelves and cover it with some rag dolls.

They all sighed with relief when the notebook showed up. That night, Isabelina and Elías sat in their bedroom, engrossed in a tense conversation, his always-present cigarette glowing in the dark. He smoked more intensely as the tale enfolded, knowing this would complicate his relationship with his best friend. He listened in silence, thinking, smoking, not saying a word. Once again, fate threatened to tear away something precious: his adored daughter.

"Let's just leave things be!" he stated tersely, bringing the matter to a close for the moment. Elías needed to be sure that Gilberto's professed friendship had not been prompted by a desire to be near his daughter. He decided to let things happen, but without seeing him as often. Besides, he felt he had no authority to question María Sucel's feelings. One thing he was certain of was that, to avoid enabling the relationship, they would stop placing their orders with El Marqués. He remembered that Eliseo had been a perfect gentleman, frankly expressing his interest in their eldest, Bertha, whom he loved devotedly.

Morning came, and Gilberto anxiously awaited Isabelina's arrival. It was a Thursday like any other in La Galería. Hours passed, and Isabelina did not come. He waited until 11:30 and decided to go out to find an explanation, for he couldn't stand to wait around any longer for news. He shuddered as he relived the feeling of loneliness that had filled him when his mother had banished him from his home. The San Francisco church bells called the faithful to noon services. Looking towards the church, he felt drawn to it to look for Isabelina there, though there was scant chance of finding her, since she usually stopped by no later than nine. Before entering, he stood in the doorway and turned around, hoping that from that higher vantage point he would be able to see her walking in the plaza. He looked intently at each person he saw, took a cigarette from the pack and lit it up, and smoked it halfway before tossing the rest of it. Inside the church, he paused in front of the rack of publications, eying them. Walking along the right side, he scanned the church carefully without seeing her, his hands in his pockets. He tossed some coins in the alms box set against one wall, and crossed himself. At the table with votive candles, he stopped and looked at them for a moment. Some women prayed in front of the candles, while others came and arranged their candles on the table, then lit them and began praying too.

He approached one of the women and quietly said, "Excuse me, ma'am."

The women looked at him with some surprise.

"Excuse me, who are you praying for?" asked Gilberto.

"I am not praying for anyone, merely giving thanks to God," she explained, and paid him no more mind as she continued her prayers.

Gilberto watched as the faithful came towards the burning candles, and after lighting their own, prayed fervently. Noticing that they were getting the candles from the sacristy, he headed there, warily wondering as he entered whether someone would stop him. The sacristan had his back towards him, standing at a table pushed against the wall, readying a swab to sprinkle holy water and an open pyx containing quite a few host wafers, a paten, a communion cup for the congregation, and the thurible for burning incense. The sacristan had not noticed Gilberto watching him until he coughed quietly to announce himself. Turning without surprise, he asked what he could do for him.

"Sir, I would like to purchase a candle, like the ones the ladies light at that little table over there," he said. He pointed without raising his hand, remembering that, when he was a child, his mother had lectured that pointing was impolite.

"Do you mean a votive?" the sacristan inquired and smiled as he indicated the amount to be paid. Holding his candle, Gilberto returned to where the small fire burned to light it. Then he took a small step away and bowed his head. Not knowing what to pray, he apologized to God, and asked for help in finding the calm he needed to withstand his despair. Afterwards, slightly comforted, he left through the atrium, went down the steps and then crossed the street to look for Don Aniceto, whom he questioned as a last resort. Gilberto finally verified that, just as he had thought, Isabelina had gone to mass as usual but had ignored him. Despondent, he returned to El Marqués.

Ophir, leaning against one of the counters as she served a client, did not hide her pleasure at seeing him. He explained that he had been on the other side of the building, negotiating with other suppliers who offered a better price for a quintal of red cranberry beans.

"Hey, Don Gilberto, you're too important to the smooth operation of this store," announced Ophir, almost shouting, her face showing a hint of coquettishness. "Don't disappear for so long ..."

"And here I thought you could fend for yourselves. So ... if I die, it's the end of El Marqués?"

"God forbid! Let El Marqués disappear, but don't let my boss die, for I will die myself," she said, laughing. Gilberto looked at her mockingly, and she continued her hilarity while her coworkers laughed at the conversation, lightening their workload.

In those days, Ophir was always trying to get the big guy to notice her, relying on her innate sauciness, which he did his best to ignore. Burdened with his thoughts, he went into a small office and sat on a stool in front of a desk covered with papers. He lit a cigarette and blew out several large puffs of smoke, as was his habit. The woman came up behind him and stroked his shoulders, while he ignored her and continued smoking. The young woman insisted, caressing him and kissing his neck repeatedly. She still couldn't get him to pay much attention to her, and he quietly moved his face away to avoid her attentions. Finally, taking hold of her arms, he stood and set her gently away from him.

"I'm a little upset, sweetie, and ... well, it'll pass," he told her. "It's best not to mess around here; we can't afford any street gossip. Think about it—if your husband were to know. And we don't need Don Juvenal to think that his business is a mess. Let's get back to work."

"God forbid! If Don Juvenal finds out, it's not so bad. But if Ulises were to even suspect that you drive me crazy with lust ... I don't even want to think about it. Ulises is a very violent man. I wish I could leave him, damn it!" she said, her eyes openly filled with hate. Gilberto couldn't help feeling fear, because his life was getting complicated just when he had set his heart on being with María Sucel. To wiggle out of the situation, he opted for patting Ophir's backside and leaving.

"Don't forget to come back, okay?" Ophir called after him, with a naughty tone.

The day began like a comedy, but one that was tumultuous and full of brawling. A battered Don Aniceto was seen crawling on all fours, half-hidden by the crowd, trying to recover some of the buns that were rolling along the sidewalk. He was surrounded by the chaos and unruliness of thousands of neighbors, some of whom, in their elation, had pushed over his sales cart. Dozens of newspapers had been flung into the air, where many yellow, blue, and red flags waved tirelessly. The crowd chanted as one, "We won! We won!" The announcement had been what the entire country had been waiting to hear, and in contrast to other revolts, this one was greeted with happy, triumphant faces.

Luckily, nobody stepped on Don Aniceto's hands, though his buns, mere crumbs now, became snacks for the pigeons from the church of San Francisco. When he heard the reason for the celebration, the old vendor thought, *who cares if this cart is broken; I'll build another tomorrow!* and he let the revelers trample his merchandise. "Today, I'll celebrate like everyone else. Viva Colombia!" he shouted, forgetting about his livelihood for the moment. Tucking his shirt back into his pants, his hair a mess, he ran and jumped as he added his voice to the shouts of "We won! We won!"

The entire country celebrated the fall of Rojas Pinilla's military rule on that Thursday in May 1957. There was also celebrating in El Marqués, but the grille curtain had been lowered at Gilberto's command. He endeavored to be a part of the celebration while also protecting the warehouse from potential vandalism and safeguarding his staff from any euphoric disruption. He considered himself a conservative and supported the future government of Guillermo León Valencia, who was touted as the most likely conservative candidate in the upcoming 1958 elections. A three-band radio was turned on, and Ophir was in charge of finding news bulletins about the situation in Bogotá as they all paid attention to the announcements.

Bogotá, UP Agency — General Gustavo Rojas Pinilla stepped down from the nation's presidency, and a military governing junta was formed with five members. It will preside over elections for the constitutional period from 1958 to 1962, in which the Colombian people will elect their president. That is the same period for which the General had been chosen...

They listened, keeping their eyes on the demonstrators outside. Ophir, no longer paying attention to the news, watched Gilberto as he commented on the situation with his employees.

"They say he hasn't left the country," a shopkeeper named Arvey said.

"But he'll have to leave, because the former presidents that he drove off will be coming back," stated Gilberto. He told everyone to go home, admonishing them to be cautious of the excessive number of drunks and people with guns mingling with the revelers. The employees were happy to be dismissed; there was plenty of the day left to spend time with family and friends.

"Are you going to let me go home by myself? What if something bad were to happen to me?" Ophir asked suggestively. Gilberto got the message. He let himself be seduced by her beauty and permitted her to stay behind. Ophir's big eyes shone expectantly, and a shiver ran up her spine. He looked through the metal curtains that protected the entrance from the demonstrators, and, seeing that nobody familiar stood outside, he told Ophir to wait for him in the back room. Pale and excited, she did as he said, and he followed her there seconds later. They were both overcome by a madness that lasted until they were sated. Gilberto rearranged his underpants, which he had not completely taken off, and buttoned up his shirt. He pulled out a black comb and fixed his hair, finishing up by tying an elegant knot in his narrow tie, which had come undone in the excitement. Ophir did what she needed to put herself to rights and look normal.

"Go, go, we mustn't be seen alone here, by anyone," exclaimed Gilberto. "I'll open the gate, and you go on out. Be very careful, because that mess out there has gotten out of hand."

"Are you still thinking about María Sucel?" she asked seductively. He didn't reply, just as he hadn't replied in the past several weeks, and ushered her out after raising waist-high a metal bar that held the gates closed. Ophir bent over, went out, and in a matter of seconds had disappeared into the crowd.

Gilberto brought the gate back down and stood at a spot that let him see what was going on. He thought for a long time about the circumstances of his life, while he watched people come and go through the bars of the gate. "Where is the woman I love? How are the Barojas faring?" he thought as he sat down comfortably, leaning back against the wall on only two legs of his stool, trying to relax his mind in that hammock-like position. The commotion outside did not disturb the silence within the store. A lit cigarette dangled from his lips, the white ashes floating down to lie on his shirt or his pants. Wrapped up in his thoughts, he was oblivious to his surroundings. His breathing occasionally became audible in the silence; one of his eyes remained half closed to avoid the smoke drifting up from the cigarette.

She turned nineteen last month, he thought.

The iron gate rattled loudly as Don Aniceto shook it excitedly; the day had become a celebration. Seeing his smiling face, Gilberto realized he should be out there and celebrating like everyone else, sensing it wouldn't really be dangerous.

"What are you doing here? Have you sold all your buns, or did you give them away?"

"Neither! I ran out of buns early today. With all these happy people, they were gone in a minute."

"Does that mean you sold them all?"

"It means I didn't sell a single one; I made a special donation to the pigeons." They chatted while the supervisor made sure that El Marqués was locked up tightly.

"And how is it that the pigeons have the pleasure of tasting your little buns today? Did you send them a kind invitation?"

"Don't they wish … Some idiot demonstrators surrounded me, oblivious of my sales cart, and with all the shoving, everything tumbled. But, well, no matter now. What's important is that we are celebrating the General's downfall. From now on, we will have no more censorship of the press, we will choose who governs us, and we will be able to live in a democracy, as we should." They went to a nearby bar and ordered beer. The woman who served them warned that they would have to pay in advance and stand while they drank their beers, because the chairs were mostly taken. They didn't stay there long, and each headed to his own home.

Gilberto left without paying much attention to the people who greeted him along the way. He walked for twenty minutes or so, letting his intuition lead the way, finally stopping at a small corner shop at the highest point of a steep neighborhood in Armenia. He'd been doing that same thing for days. It was a small place that served only coffee, some carbonated drinks, and fresh baked goods; it had only three tables, with four chairs apiece. He sat at one table that gave him a view of the whole street, keeping his eye on a specific house located on the hill at the beginning of the block. The shop owner greeted him as she dried her wet hands on a dishcloth, her face breaking into a welcoming smile. He loosened the knot in his tie as he sat. The woman didn't wait for his order, nor did he give her one; she just brought his coffee to the table. He showed her his empty cigarette box, and she returned with a new one and a book of matches. Gilberto drank the coffee slowly, carefully watching the length and breadth of the neighborhood that held his limited dreams. Realizing that he hadn't paid his bill in a while, he asked Doña Etelvina how much it totaled so far, almost embarrassed to be ordering more coffee.

"At the rate I'm going, you'll go bankrupt because of me. What do I owe you?" he asked. "Today I'll pay for all my sips of corner bitterness."

"Ha, ha, ha," the woman laughed. "I'll total it tomorrow, Don Gilberto. It's only a few daily coffees; I'm almost embarrassed to charge you for them." Doña Etelvina sat next to him, and together they began to add up almost nine months of coffee and cigarettes. When they were done, Gilberto paid her with a wad of bills he withdrew from his pocket, not counting them.

"You shouldn't pay more than you owe, Don Gilberto. I'm always very happy to serve you. Tell me, are you still despondent?"

"I've made up my mind to go right up to the door of the house and knock on it until someone comes out. If old Elías comes out, I'll say hello and ask about her. If her mother does, I'll also say hello and ask about her. And if she comes out, I'll ask her if she ever thinks of me at all."

"I can see you're still suffering. I saw her this morning; she looked quite pleased with herself, looking very nice, and her hair all done up. She wore a black skirt and a pink blouse. She looked very pretty." Gilberto remained there for over an hour, ordering several coffees, which he drank slowly as he smoked, and wrote his random thoughts on a sheet of notebook paper, borrowed from Doña Ete, as he liked to call her. *What are you doing right now at this moment? Are you thinking of me, reading a story?*

Juan de Dios

...*1969*

The doctor didn't even blink. He just stood there, relaxed, unconcerned, without clearing up any of the contradictions or trying to soothe María Sucel's troubled feelings. She had thought that things were going well with the contraceptives, but now she faced a suffocating truth.

"One can't truly determine whether the pills failed, or whether you failed. It's possible that you might have skipped a dose, or that your body ignored its effect. These things happen frequently; the most efficient contraceptive method is still abstinence," stated the doctor.

María Sucel was depressed again. Over the following week, she grieved and didn't even bothering to fix herself up to visit her friend Iphigenia. She chastised herself, thinking of all the effort she had made to go through the abortion a few months earlier. This time, she had preferred to consult the doctor who had once inspired such confidence. She sensed that it would be very dangerous to have another abortion, given how recent and traumatic it had all been. So, she returned to the doctor and asked about the risks of going forward with this pregnancy with her weakened uterus, or the dangers involved in having an abortion again so soon, with so little recovery time in between. The doctor had been unaware of the abortion and, upon hearing about it from the patient herself, preferred not to take any professional stance.

She felt more alone than ever in deciding her future. This time, there was no pinching her belly, no despair. She felt cold and had a crazy desire to have her mother near, so she could at least ask her to pray. Doña Iphigenia, already involved in the issue, was the best of friends, cheering her up and helping her get her thoughts in order. Gilberto remained unaware of the whole situation, immersed in his own enthusiasm.

After much reflection, she concluded the die had been cast, and the Cervanteses would have a second child born in the city. They'd have to think of a name.

Her belly had now grown for five months. Life in Bogotá had become more difficult for her with Gilberto spending so much time on the plains, though his remittances were timely. Rosalía became the household member who took care of all the heavy housework, such as laundry, food preparation, and childcare. As this was considered a very high-risk pregnancy and Maria Sucel's health had deteriorated noticeably, it was closely monitored by the doctor.

The new pregnancy made Gilberto quite excited; around this time, he was trying to find a place for his parents, Acasio and Sara, who had decided to come to live in Bogotá under his financial protection. Although they had a very large family, their other sons, Analdo and Sigifredo, had never managed to get well established enough financially to be able to support them. They were settled quite nicely in a tenant house near La Granja, with all their belongings. Gilberto's sister Federica, or Ñata, and the young card sharp, Sigifredo, who was so lazy he'd never let go of his parents' coattails, traveled with them, further enlarging the number of Gilberto's dependants.

Things started to get difficult around September 1967. Gilberto returned to Bogotá every weekend, trying to recover the money he had lent to Don Octavio. The man avoided him, saying he was busy, and in his stead, Doña Marina tried to alleviate the strain by creating a web of mystery and mistrust. María Sucel had become skeptical about the whole situation and had begun criticizing the relationship with the Tejadas, calling it unfair and one-sided. Gilberto's finances began to falter.

They went out one day, recalling the old times in Armenia, when they would go out every Tuesday. An amusement park had been set up in Bogotá, near the La Granja neighborhood, with exciting attractions, and they had a very good time despite María Sucel's delicate pregnancy. This first extended family outing in Bogotá was comforting. The lights and crowds created a magical feeling of togetherness and pride. There were smiles everywhere, children shouting to be heard in the midst of all the excitement. Toñito and Tomás were in charge of the little ones.

But Gilberto was nervous. He knew there would be tough days ahead, days filled with change and difficult decisions. As in the prophesied days before the final judgement, there were many things that had yet to happen, definitive things in everyone's lives. A whirlwind of situations awaited them that would tear up whatever remained of their foundations of trust and security. Deeply aware of his many woes, he couldn't help being distracted as they walked together through the amusement park, but he never avoided the glances of his family, giving each person a wide, sincere smile. María Sucel noticed his anxiety, though she dared not ask about it. She was nervous, too, feeling a strange chill in her soul that seemed to foreshadow something strange that was about to happen. Gilberto had planned this first outing spontaneously, but now he was acting strangely, though doing his best to hide it.

They all got on the carousel, thinking it would be the least dangerous ride for the children. They sat on the horses and competed to be the best rider. María Sucel sat down on a bench near one of the stalls to enjoy all the joy but never took her eyes off Gilberto. He was upset, she could tell, but making a great effort to be happy. Leaving the carousel, they overwhelmed a cotton candy vendor, emptying his stock and filling his pocket with coins. Then they stood at another stall, fascinated by an escape artist whose skill with knots left the whole family open-mouthed with amazement. Gilberto rewarded him with some coins, thinking of the metaphor for his own life presented in the show, where, against all odds, the artist had set himself free. Reflecting on his problems, he comforted himself by taking in the children's happy faces, letting their joy wash over him.

When María Sucel asked him, "Do you love me?" he smiled and acted offended, secretly surprised and pleased, and replied that he loved her with all his heart and kissed her forehead. They walked along without taking their eyes off the children, who were fluttering about, asking for coins to buy all sorts of trinkets. At the Hall of Mirrors, they took a moment to sit where they could maintain complete control over the children as they enjoyed watching their little bodies be twisted and deformed in the mirrors. The laughter never stopped. The couple linked arms and inclined their heads together; he stroked her huge belly, and so they sat for several minutes.

"This is ideally the way we should live. All that traveling is so sad ... it would be good if you would live here with us all the time," she said.

He agreed, saying the plains were better suited to spiritism than to sales.

"The children always cry for you to be here, and so do I."

Gilberto did not reply. He kissed her hair again, and carelessly let slip a cold comment. "Don Octavio has been avoiding me because I'm demanding he pay back the money I lent him."

She turned serious. "Money? What money?" she challenged.

"The savings we brought from Armenia," he replied, looking dejected, turning his head towards his children to avoid looking at her.

She moved away from him and, looking at her children, asked, "Our children's tiny inheritance?"

He ducked his head and said not a word. She rose and walked to where the children were playing, her face bathed in tears. She then decided that she didn't want them to see her cry, and she especially didn't want to ruin their enjoyment, so she went back to her husband to ask when they would be paid.

"Is that Mr. Tejada, whom you consider to be God himself, an honest man? What documents did they sign?"

"None," he answered quietly.

"How could we have fallen so low? Our children will be the ones to suffer the consequences. I feel they'll never have a roof of their own over their heads. And you, what do you think you will do?"

"I don't know," he said. And for several days, silence reigned.

Gilberto went back to the plains, hoping to get his life straightened out. He returned because it was his responsibility, but there was no news about the Tejadas. They had disappeared into thin air, it seemed, and their absolute silence was concerning. The following morning, he was reviewing accounts in the warehouse when there was a loud banging on the metal curtain that acted as the door. He pulled it open and saw a number of uniformed officers, who confirmed his name and then asked him to accompany them to the police station. Gilberto went willingly, full of questions. He had the feeling that something very dark was happening that involved the Tejadas and their unexpected disappearance. He knew, however, that he had always acted with complete honesty and had never taken a penny from anyone.

When they arrived, one of the men, apparently the highest ranking, ushered Gilberto into his office and cordially informed him that they had been investigating the Tejadas for several years. They were being sought by the authorities, accused of fraud, criminal association, and major embezzlement. Gilberto also learned that they were part of a criminal network, using a restaurant in Bogotá as their headquarters, pretending to be spiritists to defraud people from every social class. They also sold merchandise smuggled from Venezuela, illegally brought through La Guajira. As part of the same operation, the police had dismantled a cell in Armenia and had freed a woman one of the criminals, named Ulises Calzada, a.k.a. "Rabbit," had been keeping as a slave. Using death threats against her and her loved ones, he had been coercing her to commit crimes, stealing money from businessmen and tradesmen, that was then handed over to criminal groups. When Gilberto heard the name Ulises, he asked the police about the woman and was told she was one Ophir Garrido, who was now under the protection of the authorities in Armenia, due to continued death threats. He learned that Ulises was in hiding and that the authorities had a warrant for his arrest.

All this information plunged Gilberto into such despair that his legs wobbled and his stomach cramped with sudden diarrhea that he struggled anxiously to contain. This was the third time he had felt this way, after the robbery of their home and the holdup on the day they were leaving for Bogotá. His drama, begun so many years earlier, continued to smolder, but now into this huge problem he was dragging his wife and his children, and even Ophir. Until that moment, he had tried to bury her in his mind as the most treacherous of his lovers, an enemy. He pitied her and was terrified. Again, the contradictions surfaced. He wondered whether Ophir had ever really loved him, or if she had loved him but could not stop hurting him, or if, if, if ... While he stood guiltless before the law, he involuntarily thought of what this would mean for his children and of María Sucel. He felt abused.

He began telling his own story, explaining to the authorities his relationship with Ophir. Thus, Gilberto Cervantes-Cervantes and Ophir Garrido became key witnesses in the investigation and trial against those criminals. In other words, more problems. The officer questioned him for almost two hours. Luckily, he was not incriminated; the ongoing investigations indicated to the authorities that Gilberto had acted honestly.

But he had lost everything. He was forced to stay in the plains and work for the next few weeks, collecting payment of pending invoices from the many clients that only he knew about. However, those funds would be confiscated, and he would receive only an adjusted fee.

After that, Gilberto did not immediately return to Bogotá, for he had agreed with the police to help them learn more about Ophir. Like him, she was a protected witness who must remain under observation until Ulises was arrested. He was again filled with hope that part of his money might be recovered, and, taking a chance, asked if he could visit her where she was staying. The authorities agreed, but warned that they would be monitoring him due to the risks involved and that someone would have to be present during their conversation. Another condition, maybe the most important one, was that she would have to agree to the meeting. Gilberto agreed to the terms and had expressly requested that the authorities keep his family and friends in Bogotá unaware of the entire investigation. In view of the circumstances, and in consideration of his status as an unindicted witness, the authorities assured him that it would be so. He was able to breathe easier, at least for the moment.

He traveled to Armenia through Bogotá, a trip that took twelve straight hours. The authorities had indicated that he would stay at a hotel, and once he had registered at the front desk, they would provide instructions. It was a hotel he was very familiar with, for he had often had sexual encounters with Ophir at that very same place. He had been there for a day and hadn't dared go down to the lobby for fear of being recognized. Having arrived at dawn, he had seen nobody since his arrival except the bellhop, a man he had repeatedly had contact with in the past. Ophir was brought to the room at about two in the afternoon that day, accompanied by an officer—a large, friendly young woman. She arrived looking like Sophia Loren in the magazines, when she was trying to avoid photographers. A dark scarf covered her head, and she was wearing dark glasses. It was a look he really liked. Ophir seemed happy to see him and smiled openly. Despite the mess of circumstances that had brought them together, he was happy to see her. They looked at each other for a minute.

"Hello, Ophir. How are you?" Gilberto asked tentatively.

"As you can see, running from life itself," she replied, expelling all the air trapped in her lungs.

"Here, go ahead and sit down, here on the bed, for they won't give us much time," he urged, getting serious. He had had many lonely hours since leaving Villavicencio to think about the things he wanted to ask her. However, he couldn't help noticing how beautiful she still was, though she was thinner than he remembered. Ophir approached the bed nervously, exuding a strange smell. Gilberto sensed that she was under a lot of pressure, and to lighten the mood, he took a chair that was next to a small table and offered it to the woman on duty.

"Please sit, officer. How much time will we have to talk?" he asked respectfully.

"About twenty minutes, maybe a bit more," the guard replied without looking at him.

"Everything that has happened has been terrible. Now

we're poor, sad, and without much hope," he said, referring to Ophir.

"It's true," she exclaimed, falling to her knees in front of him, and wailing. "This is the life that we were given. I am so sorry for everything that has happened, but I can't stop loving you! I can't, no matter how much I try," she repeated, quite overcome.

"Stand up, Ophir, I don't want us to suffer anymore. Calm down, and tell me everything," he told her, stooping to help her up.

"They forced me to go along with them. They threatened to kill me, and to kill you, if things didn't go well. When Ulises realized that I was truly in love with you, he focused on hurting us both as much as he could. You don't know how I've suffered about all this, Gilberto dear," Ophir confessed sadly while sobbing, as he watched her and tried to find some honesty in all that drama.

"I did everything Ulises asked of me. That's why I followed you to El Paraíso, so I could tell him about all the things you had in your home. I had to tell him everything, so he wouldn't kill us. When I heard about the robbery, I was in such pain. I didn't know they would do that," she admitted emotionally. "He forced me to get your money and give it to him. That nefarious man only used us. He was tangled up with a much larger gang. They had a lot of people like me; they forced them to do the same as I did. Many times, they killed people who wouldn't cooperate, and they would tell me about it to frighten me. It's true, even if you don't believe me. I have been truly in love with you, Gilberto, and I did everything I could to protect you. When you decided to leave for Bogotá, they already knew that you were taking money with you and decided to rob you. I didn't tell them. It wasn't me—it was someone from Bogotá who told them. I don't know too much about that, because by then things with Ulises were pretty bad. When I heard, I wanted to kill him, but he was the one who almost killed me. That's when I decided to run away. I heard that you had gone to Bogotá, partly to try to hide the truth about us for so many years."

Gilberto couldn't believe it. He was hearing a pathetic story, full of suffering and hopelessness. Ophir seemed sincere and looked very upset. Maybe each one had seen the other as a lighthouse amid all the dark uncertainty.

"I've come to ask you about the money you were holding for me," said Gilberto, knowing the answer. Ophir couldn't look at him, and was silent. "Did you give it to Ulises, too?" he insisted, and she nodded.

"Forgive me, Gilberto, for the love of God! Forgive me! If I hadn't, we'd all be dead. You, me, María Sucel, and possibly even your children. They've already killed many people in Quindío. People like you, like me."

There was little left to say. Gilberto turned to the officer and pointed out that they had used up their twenty minutes. "Thank you very much, ma'am, for accompanying Ophir to this appointment." The woman did not reply, but she pressed her lips together, surely sad over everything she had heard.

"I'm very sorry for everything that happened to us; I'm happy we're still alive. Be careful of Ulises. He's the worst kind of thug, but you already know that. I wish you well," he sincerely told his old lover.

"All I ask is that you forgive me, for the love of God," repeated Ophir firmly, but sorrowfully and quietly. "That is the only thing that would comfort my soul. So help me God and the Virgin Mary, I want to prove to you that I've always been a good woman, and never stopped loving you." Gilberto didn't say a word, just listened to her respectfully. Ophir turned away and asked the officer if they could leave.

Gilberto returned to Villavicencio, just as he had agreed with the authorities, going over in his mind everything that had happened to him. He chose to set all of these events aside and began to polish his idea of becoming an independent salesman in Bogotá. He would work on his own, starting with some borrowed merchandise, and he wouldn't have a boss, and he wouldn't trust anyone other than himself. Gilberto knew his finances were in ruins, and that it would affect his entire family. He thought of his wife, in advanced stages of pregnancy, and was glad that she had not been a part of all these bad things.

In the meantime, María Sucel had already arranged with Berenice, the same midwife who had delivered Acasio Elías, to deliver Juan de Dios in early January 1978, although the doctor recommended that the birth take place in a maternity clinic. Gilberto arrived at the capital in November, thrilled to see his children and feel Juan de Dios kicking inside his wife's bulky belly.

Despite the current circumstances, Gilberto was as excited as he had always been when María Sucel had a baby. At the time, the little ones were on their school break and were home all day. He planned, some three months after the delivery was done with, to tell my mother the whole story, tell her how Octavio Tejada had stolen the money, because he had turned out to be a swindler together with his wife, and that's why they were already in jail. In other words, he would tell her a story that she could deem fair and true. For now, he would keep the rest of the facts in other compartments in his mind, in another of his exiles, forever or at least indefinitely.

The trial continued to be a pending issue, however. Gilberto would have to present himself at the Paloquemao courthouse in Bogotá to testify during that whole month. He would do so, knowing that María Sucel could never know about it. This was one more thing for him to worry about as he pushed forward bravely.

During the first day of the trial, he watched Ophir all the time, and he felt her watching him without mercy. As she was a star witness in the investigation, they were keeping her hidden away in some hotel in Bogotá, at least until the trial was over and she was declared innocent of all charges. Those encounters with Ophir during the trial had a great impact on him. He heard from many sources, or witnesses, about how savagely she had been abused and how Ulises, who was still at large, had forced her to commit crimes. He remembered the last words Ophir had said to him in the hotel in Armenia, and was touched. She had sworn that she still loved him, that she had always loved him. Gilberto knew he was weak in these matters, matters of the heart. During one of the breaks, on the second day of the trial, he decided to go and talk to her, because he saw she was alone and thought she might be sad, maybe cold. He thought that she wasn't used to the cold of Bogotá, or to the city, or to the apparent rudeness of the people, especially in the middle of such a challenging situation as a trial.

"How do you feel?" he asked her.

"Sad, but hoping to be released. Free of all this shit that has stuck to me in life," she said, clearly much affected by the circumstances.

"Are you also referring to me?"

"No, not you. Why would I say that? You, too, have been stained by all the rottenness surrounding me. I only hope for it all to end; then I'll see what I'll do," she said, without waiting for Gilberto to ask her what she planned to do with her life.

"Will you go back to Armenia?"

"How can you say that, Gilberto?" she replied indignantly. "With Ulises at large, there's no way I can go to Armenia, or Montenegro, or Quimbaya, or anywhere at all in Quindío. That area is the worst place, a hellhole, for me. I must disappear and forget about—"

"So, where will you go?"

"They will let me stay in the hotel where they have me for a month, I think, because they think they'll be able to catch Ulises. Afterwards, I'll have to decide what to do. Right now, I don't know. We'll see."

"So ... what hotel is it?"

"The San Diego Garden. It's a small but very comfortable and elegant hotel. The food is good, though they don't serve beans with pork rinds or sliced plantains. Yesterday, I asked for *mazamorra*, and they brought me sweet cooked maize; I think they call it *peto*."

"What do you do to pass the time?"

"I don't do anything, for now. I stay in bed, listening to the news on the radio, when I'm not listening to music. I keep hoping to hear something about Armenia. I don't know ... I have the feeling that, maybe, I'll hear something good at some point, because everything I hear and see is bad. That's what I think," she said, and her eyes filled with tears again.

"Everything will turn out all right. ... Let's stay strong, and then nobody else will suffer," Gilberto suggested to cheer her up.

"We'll see," she said.

He didn't ask her anything else, and, feeling very discouraged, she preferred not to add anything more to the conversation, either. They were quiet again, and in their silence, each gesture or movement became more noticeable and eloquent. They discreetly stole glimpses of each other until they were called to the judge's chambers. Gilberto thought again about María Sucel. He knew he was a wretch; he held in his hands the happiness of two women, women who had led parallel lives to earn his love. His absent wife, still an angel and mother of almost eight of his children. Ophir, in love with him and, having never borne children, still looking youthful and fiery, her gaze challenging and passionate. In his confusion, he felt helpless to distinguish between love and lust. And, with terror, he realized that perhaps he had never known how. Maybe he felt true love for María Sucel, but, at this point, what did he feel for Ophir? He couldn't help seeing that Ophir was still very pretty, though less seductive than before. In his heart, he felt infinite empathy with her suffering, even though, however unintentionally, she had drawn him into the maze in which he now found himself. He wished he had asked her to explain more about how it all happened, but it seemed morbid to make her recall the intimate details of events that were so filled with malice.

That was when, from his other exile, from his spiritism, he drew forth kindness and reminded himself of his own values. He concluded that in a different life, they must have suffered a traumatic death or something of that sort, and for that reason, their spirits were uneasy and suffering in this world. Gilberto thought and thought about this and decided that both he and Ophir were good spirits who were being used by other, very low-level, evil spirits, prevailing on earth.

When he arrived home, María Sucel noted how tense and distracted he seemed. She pampered him, serving him tidbits of food she had prepared. Ironically, they were similar to those she'd offered the day Ophir had visited her, just before that fateful robbery. Gilberto thanked her, and, unusually insistent, said he must pray for a woman who was suffering in Bogotá. She understood, so he closed himself off in the small sanctuary and prayed for her and for himself. While he was praying, Ophir was staring at the four walls of her hotel room, trying to ward off the Bogotá cold that seemed to permeate her skin and sink into her very organs. She felt very alone and abandoned, though Gilberto was hoping, with his prayers, to send her a good spirit to keep her company.

sDays passed and the trial continued. Gilberto regularly shared breaks in the courthouse with Ophir, and there developed between them a new level of trust, framed this time by mutual solidarity. The woman had managed, maybe intentionally, to get her former lover to tacitly forgive her and forget everything that had happened. With just a week remaining in the month that the authorities had set aside for her protection and Ulises still not captured, anxiety once again became their daily routine. Gilberto now felt the need to participate actively in Ophir's protection; she would be forced to stay somewhere anonymous in Bogotá due to the circumstances. He felt responsible again, repeating the role of good person that he'd played his entire life. She would once again depend on him, just as his parents did, and his wife and all his children. The most pressing problem continued to be his financial situation, since a whole new world of needs and demands was looming.

"What a surprise!" exclaimed María Sucel, with some hope, "Now that I think of it, we left Armenia without saying goodbye to her. This house is nothing like our palace in El Paraíso, but it's clean. We could offer her some Santa Fe chocolate, and Don Alirio's good bread. She'll surely bring a letter from my mother ..."

Ophir arrived that afternoon. Gilberto went to pick her up from where she was supposedly staying with relatives in the capital. Upon her arrival, the cordiality exceeded expectations. In her discomfort, María Sucel became an excellent hostess. They talked extensively about Armenia. Night fell, the shadows filled with a cold wind. In the empty streets, the only people to be seen were walking swiftly towards their warm homes after getting off a bus. At ten, there was discussion about whether Ophir should return to her relatives' home that same night, or if the Cervantes family would offer her a place to stay. While his wife suggested their guest would be very uncomfortable, Gilberto pretended he would go along with whatever the ladies chose. The fact was that it was Ophir's decision whether she wished to stay, despite the discomfort. After accepting to stay, they discussed who would sleep in which bed. For now, with Rosalía, the family numbered ten, and Ophir made eleven. In the end, they decided that Acasio Elías would sleep with Rosalía, and Gilberto would sleep on the right in the marriage bed, María Sucel in the middle, and Ophir on the left side. He would take her back to her lodgings on the following day. It was a cheerful evening; the children fell asleep, and the three adults sat up chatting before going to bed. María Sucel lent her friend a robe, and they slept. In the morning, Rosalía served breakfast, and Ophir bid her hostess goodbye, promising to give her regards to Isabelina.

The last of the Cervantes children was born on January 11, 1969; it was a boy, and they named him Juan de Dios. The child arrived in a house overrun with stacks of all kinds of merchandise, which left barely any space between the beds and only narrow passages to walk through. Even the bathroom had merchandise piled in it, and in a space that joined the patio with the main bedroom and the kitchen, the metal cart was parked, with a bicycle named "La Burra" that could carry any amount of weight on its rear fender. It had become apparent that their financial situation was unsustainable, and all his dependents requested miracles that were difficult to fulfill: Don Acasio and Doña Sara on one hand, Ophir on the other; and of course María Sucel and the children. Their lack of repayment was straining Don Antonio's willingness to help them by carrying their debt.

In the midst of the whole mess that was Gilberto's life, the "truth" he told María Sucel was that the Tejadas had let him go a while ago, no longer needing his services because he had told him he wanted to branch off on his own. He had achieved that independence, but his wife continued to be ignorant of their true financial tragedy.

At the end of each day of sales, he had begun to park his car in front of a certain restaurant, where he drank a cup of coffee while resting his feet. This time, the coffee was followed by nine beers, which made him unquestionably drunk. He stayed there several hours, thinking about his life, where each brick that helped to form the walls closing in on him had a specific name. His crazed mind took him back.

He remembered his beloved Nélida and her son, his son, who would be about twenty-seven now. He didn't know him because he had lost track of him when he was still little, due to one of those things. Arriving home, he stumbled as he pushed his heavy cart, and it took a long while before he was able, with Antonio's help, to store it on the small patio. Silently, he covered the cart with plastic, then went to the bedroom, where his children played by climbing over the merchandise, while his wife took care of the newborn baby. Realizing he was drunk, María Sucel felt tenderness for him.

"There will be no cooking in this house tonight," Gilberto announced. "I brought grilled chicken, with corncakes and salted potatoes. Tell Rosalía to cut it up for the children and for us; and if it's not enough to fill our bellies, she should let me know, because I have a lot of money, enough to buy all the grilled chicken in Bogotá." He took a fistful of wrinkled bills from his pocket and showed María Sucel. Then he sat on the edge of the bed where little Juan de Dios babbled restlessly, and burst into tears. María Sucel, seeing him so depressed, covered his face with kisses, and the children came and surrounded him with affection, forcing him to eat something.

Three months passed, the debts piled up, and Gilberto continued to drink. A woman in Chapinero offered María Sucel day work, washing clothes in a concrete sink and ironing them, for minimal wages, but he would not allow it. They were behind on their rent, and various everyday items began to go missing from their lives.

Page Nine Hundred Seventy...

...1958

Isabelina got up from the couch, setting aside the knitting needles she was using to knit little Myriam a cotton jacket, and went to answer the door. She opened it to find a boy of about eleven holding a bouquet of tuberoses wrapped in tissue paper. The boy asked for María Sucel.

"A man sent these for her," stated the boy, as he pointed up the hill. Isabelina stepped forward and looked towards Doña Ete's store. Her hands flew to her mouth when she realized it was Gilberto looking back at her. Confused, she stared at the infamous bouquet and asked the boy to wait. Those tuberoses screamed at her that the man had his mind set on taking up his place again in the Barojas' lives. Leaving the door open, she walked slowly back towards the kitchen, where María Sucel was peeling plantains, and quietly told her what was happening. Heavy with uncertainty, she sat down in a small armchair next to the breakfast table and covered her mouth again anxiously, seeing the bewilderment on her daughter's face as she walked to the front door.

"These flowers are for you, from that man over

there," said the boy as he pointed up the hill. María Sucel thanked him and took the flowers resolutely. Instinctively, she bent her head to smell their fragrance, though frowning in consternation. The boy left, and she looked up the hill, anxious to make out the sender. As Isabelina had a moment earlier, she recognized Gilberto. When he lifted his hand, she did the same and looked at the tuberoses as if seeing them for the first time. Then she shut the door and walked through the house, perplexed. After placing the flowers on the dining room table, she sat down on a chair and clutched her hair, taking deep breaths, her forehead etched. She dropped her head to her knees and remained in that position for a few moments, finally lifting her eyes to look at the tuberoses again. Picking them up carefully, she went to the kitchen, where Isabelina was still sitting in the armchair. María Sucel washed the vase and filled it halfway with water, then arranged the bouquet, trimming the stems a bit with her sewing scissors. Finally her slim fingers pulled from them the most beautiful petal to take to her room. Taking her notebook from the cabinet, she wrote down the date and, sniffing the petal's aroma again, she tucked away the pale, silky token of love.

Elías, who had been out running some errands, came back a while later. His good mood disappeared when he saw the flowers. He looked for Isabelina, to blame her; overcome with jealousy, he went to their room and shouted for her. "Isabelina!"

"Don't answer him, please, Mother. I'll explain about the flowers," María Sucel said boldly, but Isabelina stood and went to find her husband.

"He's back, isn't he?" Elías asked.

"I'd say he's never left."

"He dared to knock on our door!" he exclaimed angrily, and cursed the man. "The girl won't be happy. That's what irritates me the most."

The impertinent flowers continued to arrive twice a week. The young woman couldn't find a place to put them anymore, and Gilberto continued watching in the evenings from Doña Etelvina's shop. The regular deliveries brought great tension into the Baroja home, trying the patience of each family member.

When Isabelina returned from church one morning, she noticed that María Sucel hadn't left her room yet. Finding her bundled in bed, covered from head to toe, she shook her shoulder gently, thinking she might be ill. The girl had been awake for a while and flipped off the covers, unable to hide her grim face.

"What time is it, mother?" she asked.

"It's almost ten, but don't worry, dear, I'll take care of your tasks," replied Isabelina. Hoping she'd stay under the covers, she promised to pamper her. To fortify her, she prepared some *caspiroleta*, with warm milk, plenty of eggs and some white wine. She suggested they go for a walk later in the fields, to breathe the cool air that came down from the mountains and talk, like two adult women taking the time to be friends and share the day's beauty. She told her they would pick geraniums or bougainvillea, listen to mockingbirds and cardinals, and watch the turtledoves cuddle, and was pleased to see María Sucel's face slowly lose its misery. Isabelina tucked the covers around her again, closed the shutters so no light filtered in, and closed the door as she left. She was convinced she would be able to help her daughter resist the pressure put on her by the tuberoses, roses, chrysanthemums, and geraniums.

That afternoon, they went for the walk, carrying a small basket covered with a cloth they had embroidered themselves. It was packed with snacks: a canteen full of fresh maize beverage made that morning and other delicacies Isabelina had prepared. After ten minutes, they arrived at a coffee plantation, rows of plants clustered in the shade of green clumps of plantain trees. In the distance, they could see the *chapoleras* and the bean pickers, and farther still the two-story houses with balcony railings woven of palm stems, adorned with hanging baskets and flowering bougainvillea, with some barking dogs rounding out the landscape. At that time of year, the coffee trees were full of small white flowers that seemed to twinkle on the dark green bushes bursting with red berries. The splendor of the landscape filled their hearts, almost as if they had never seen anything like it in their lives. There they paused. Smoothing her pleated skirt behind her thighs to prevent it from wrinkling, the daughter knelt, then sat calmly in front of her mother. A more formal conversation began as Isabelina took her daughter's hands and spoke to her frankly, as adult women do. She told her that love also brings despair, and that despair often hounds women in love. María Sucel listened, confused, but after a few minutes a timid smile flickered on her face. Gradually she became more intrigued.

"Love is a bitter road?" she asked, still with sadness.

"No, daughter. To love is a divine gift that sometimes hurts, wounds the soul, and battles with common sense."

"Love hurts?"

"We cause pain when we prevent love from flourishing."

"I don't understand what you're trying to say," she replied.

"The selfishness your father carries in his blood is a fruit of the love he feels for you, dear. His great love has caused bitterness in everyone. However, that bitterness will never be greater than the happiness that love will bring you." Wistfully, María Sucel cried silently. Her huge brown eyes were awash with tears that rolled down her face, slow as a moon rise. They both sat in silence for a long time. "When you wrote that acrostic four years ago, hidden in the shopping list, we thought that you were just playing around. But now, with the return of the flowers, we are forced to understand the essence of your love."

María Sucel was stunned by this confession. She had never imagined, not for a moment, that her mother had known about the acrostic, much less her father. "Gilberto read you the acrostic?" she asked, with hope, and Isabelina nodded. For the first time, hope was blossoming in María Sucel's mind that her love might be mutual, and she took a calm breath. The conversation became more emotional as they spoke for the first time about feelings. The young woman asked about when her parents were young and fell in love, as though seeking parallels.

"Times have changed," said Isabelina. "Today it's possible to dream about love, because before, marriage was more about the parents' convenience."

"How sad that must have been!" exclaimed María Sucel.

"That was how I met your sister Bertha's father, but I fell in love with old Elías."

Back at their house, the girl quietly looked for her father and found him standing at the edge of the patio, his eyes on the mountaintops that were gently graying from the fog coming off the bare uplands. Lost in thought, he felt the cool wind gently stroking him as it came down from the peaks and carried away the smoke from his cigarette. The peacefulness of the moment was disturbed when he coughed up phlegm and spit it into a clump of grass.

"Some coffee, father?" she interrupted his thoughts.

"Make it two, dear. Pour one for yourself and come keep me company. This cool sunset cannot be wasted." María Sucel returned with two cups and gave him one. "It smells wonderful, dear. The coffee from this land smells wonderful."

"It smells like coffee, Papa," she scolded in jest.

"Yes, daughter. I should say that it smells like the land's perfume," said Elías, smiling at María Sucel's words.

"Well, in some way, it is," she agreed. They settled on two chairs that looked out over the yard. Unlike other days, today her father looked rested. It seemed that something had changed in him, and the girl liked the new attitude so much that she tried to enjoy it. The old man's arm came all the way around her, and his rough, worn hand settled her head on his chest. They recalled when, as a little girl, she waited for him to come home, so she could sit on his lap and feel pampered. This was the first time she'd done so since she had grown into a young woman.

"When someone my age becomes grumpy and has no patience or humility, it's because his heart is pumping merely to move his body, not his soul," said Elías, trying to explain his surly behavior towards her and his wife over recent days. He complained that life had forced him to spend more time thinking of what he was losing with the passing of the years, instead of enjoying them. He expressed regret for his actions and revealed his sadness over recent family events, including Bertha's marriage to Eliseo, which had hit him very hard.

"I have never noticed how beautiful your eyes are, dear," Elías tenderly confessed, attempting to make her feel good. She thanked him.

"Papa, if I ask your forgiveness for all the bitter moments you've had because of me, will that be enough to ensure your affection for the rest of my life?"

Elías stared out at the horizon, and after a while, turned to look at her. "I love you very much, too, and always will," he replied. "You're a good girl. How could I not love you, and what is there to forgive, if you've never done anything improper?"

María Sucel sighed and was noticeably pale as she licked her lips to calm her nerves before asking him her next question.

"Papa. Has Gilberto been something improper that fate put in our way, to cause us so much distress?" she asked in despair. "Because of him, my life is so mixed up."

"Gilberto is a great person," Elías responded, sad and quiet, smiling in understanding.

"Don't be miserable because of me, Papa, it's not worth it," she said, overcome with bitterness. "You mustn't grow old filled with sadness because of me. On the contrary, you deserve to enjoy peace! I will no longer think of him. I will continue to ignore him."

Elías waved his hand in a gesture of denial; he didn't think this was fair. Instead, he told her he knew about the notebook filled with flower petals, and implied that he would not be the one to shut it closed. As he drank another cup of coffee, he asked her to show her herbarium to him.

Isabelina had been watching them furtively from inside the kitchen, her heart full of compassion. Seeing their faces reflecting mutual understanding at last, she recalled all her prayers and novenas, to which she attributed this harmony. She dried her tears and continued to watch them from afar, unwilling to break the spell of their private moment. As she finished sipping her coffee, she observed wistfully the prophetic designs left by the grounds at the bottom of the cup.

Myriam arrived, distracting her. "Let's go, honey, and put on your new pink dress that we bought for Sunday mass," she told her, and the little girl skipped away happily.

In Armenia's Cathedral of the Immaculate Virgin, in November 1957, Father Andreino Henao officiated at the wedding of Gilberto Cervantes-Cervantes and María Sucel Baroja Sánchez. The matrimonial registry, with the number ten stamped in gold on its cover, was open and one could clearly read the ceremony recorded there: Page 972, Registration Number 4,148. To the beggars and to the people who frequently prayed at the church, the ceremony might have seemed uneventful. But not so for a woman sitting on a wooden pew in one corner, who lingered there to watch the happy attendees as they left the church. She approached the crowd cautiously, covering her mouth with her mantle. The bride smiled at everyone; the groom enjoyed all the congratulations offered by well-wishers as they hugged him, one by one. At one point, he looked around for María Sucel, who had lingered behind for an instant, and discovered behind her the enigmatic presence of the beautiful Ophir, staring at him reproachfully. The speechless Gilberto's face revealed his discomfort. She showed herself for a long moment, looking spectacular as always, then melted into the crowd, leaving him dangling like a fish on a hook.

The newlyweds settled in a quiet neighborhood in Armenia called El Paraíso, where he had built a house with his own hands together with Don Juvenal, who was the owner of El Marqués and Gilberto's boss. It was a pleasant neighborhood, surrounded by a magical landscape. The adjacent land was carpeted with prosperous coffee plantations reaching to the bottom of a canyon that formed its boundary.

Despite the discomfort of her advanced pregnancy, his wife looked radiantly happy. With only a few weeks left before the birth of her first son, the baby's layette was ready, supplemented by gifts from the entire family. In the middle of a financial boom, Gilberto had been able to buy neighboring coffee plantations, earning additional income by selling the harvest to nearby mills. It was an enviable life, filled with activity. The landscape, their friends, their comfort, and the climate foretold the best of futures, despite fears in Colombia's government regarding a potential drop in coffee prices. According to Gilberto, these times were only relatively peaceful, because the rise of groups of bandits had begun to concern the authorities. Occasional flare-ups of communism in the country's universities did not affect the solidity of traditional political parties. After the not-so-distant times of the military dictatorship headed by Rojas Pinilla, those parties were lifesavers during elections.

Exactly nine months after the wedding, the Cervantes-Barojas' firstborn breathed the air of the coffee-growing region. Amid the entire family's admiration, he arrived, very proud of himself, on July 30th, 1958. María Sucel gave birth in her own home, assisted by the nurse from Social Services, who was a quite reputable midwife. He was baptized Antonio, apparently at the request of Gilberto, who I believe had lost a bet with a friend because the baby was a boy. It seems everything had indicated that it would be a girl, since María Sucel's belly had been large and pointy. Only five months later, she began having bouts of nausea and dizziness. Isabelina declared that her fertile body had been inseminated once again and would receive new blessings. Groceries arrived in duplicate from El Marqués to their home, and María Sucel devotedly designated part of them for her parents and even left some aside for poor folk who came knocking at the door, seeking help or scraps of food.

The young mother never went to El Marqués. In almost two years of marriage, she had been there only a couple of times, thinking that the supervisor's wife should not come to his workplace, where there were so many men. On one Monday in January 1959, El Marqués was full, and the employees could barely keep up, totaling sums for the long market lists. Gilberto was undoubtedly the most skillful at arithmetic. Clients who checked the employees' sums often found mistakes, which he resolved while chatting with them in a friendly manner to avoid disruption. His experience and people skills had made him an old hand at this.

In the middle of the busy workday, a fascinating face emerged from the crowd, one whose appearance Gilberto found bittersweet and challenging. The kind of face that, despite having neither aroma nor taste, can make a man salivate. That face crossed in front of Gilberto's eyes unexpectedly, giving him no time to react, and asked if he needed help with the customers. Surprised, he couldn't help feeling a strange vibration in his belly. Those dazzling eyes cornered him in the darkest of his mental labyrinths. It was Ophir, dressed in black and wearing a red shawl, showing off her curves all the way to her calves.

"Hello, sugar, do you need help?" she asked coquettishly.

Gilberto swallowed, his face pale and his brow tense. Only a couple of seconds had gone by when he answered, almost as a reflex, "Hello, no, um ... that's not necessary. How are you?"

"Fine. I decided to come and place my order in

person," replied Ophir.

"All right, fine, we'll be with you shortly," he said, pretending he was busy with one of the orders. However, their last moments together were passing through his mind: the erstwhile adulteress weeping as they bid farewell, and that last time in the cathedral, on his wedding day. Ophir's return now didn't make any sense, and it was driving him toward a sickening panic. He was hoping the encounter was just coincidence, but the suggestive dress and the red shawl seemed to contradict that. In despair, he tried to conjure up María Sucel's face as a protective shield. He didn't want to allow any thoughts that would let his libido detour him towards memories of fleeting sex in the tiny office. Ophir was so attractive that it was impossible to ignore her. It just so happened that none of the men working that day had known her from years ago.

Thinking of María Sucel made him respond, and while the mysterious visitor watched him closely, he discreetly approached an employee and murmured, "Take care of the customer in red. Stick to her and do what you can, so she leaves quickly."

"Yes, sir, boss," the man replied and went to help her.

"I'd like your boss to take care of my list. I'd rather wait," she said when the man approached, and she smiled sarcastically.

"Don Gilberto asked me to help you, so you don't have to wait so long."

"All right. You begin filling my order, but I prefer that he be the one to add up my bill," she insisted. A few minutes passed, while customers chatted as they waited for their orders to be filled. A woman came in holding two bunches of freshly cut flowers. Squeezing through the crowd, she caught Gilberto's attention as he picked up and packed groceries to avoid having to look at Ophir.

"Here are the flowers, Don Gilberto, and they're prettier

than usual," she said. Gilberto looked at her pleasantly, but his eyes couldn't help straying towards the woman in the shawl. He knew she understood perfectly that the flowers were for someone they both knew. Ophir covered her mouth and smiled thinly, lowering her eyes. Gilberto looked back at the flowers and chose some tuberoses, pulled some bills from his pocket and paid the vendor, thanking her. Setting the flowers to one side on the counter, he continued working.

Ophir took the opportunity to annoy him. Noting that his back was turned so he wouldn't see her, she took the flowers and walked to the bathroom, where she filled a small bucket with water from the faucet and placed the flowers inside. On her way back, she paused briefly as she walked past the small office, checking out the walls and desk where they had enjoyed each other more than a few times. Gilberto, no longer seeing her in the store, thought she had left and was surprised when he saw her come out from the back.

"It's not fair for María Sucel's flowers to be wilted when they arrive," she teased, more seductive than ever. Listening to her, Gilberto's mind roiled, and for a moment he remembered her—panting, possessed, dominated, wild as an untamed animal, crazed to the point of letting her passion guide her actions.

"You shouldn't have come in here, and you shouldn't have taken the flowers!" he shouted, feeling trapped by the circumstances. She ignored this exclamation, as though it didn't matter. Then his face reddened and he lost his composure, along with any semblance of clear-headedness, and he berated his employee.

"Palomino, customers are not allowed inside the store past the counter, not even for personal favors … Is this lady's order ready?"

"Yes, boss, it's all packed; here's the list. I've already added it up, but she asked me to have you do it." Gilberto totaled the bill and told his employee to charge her.

Ophir paid the bill, but, before leaving the warehouse, spoke again to him. "My husband has left me. I'm alone now, and free of sins," she whispered. Gilberto was speechless, left hanging.

The workday ended, and his thoughts fluttered around like a caged sparrow. Arriving home after nine that night, and after hugging María Sucel and covering Toñito with kisses, he dropped onto the couch, intending to relax. But he couldn't keep his eyes off the vase filled with flowers that secretly carried the imprint of a past permeated by Ophir.

An Old Rattletrap Bus

...*1959*

A quiet day after the rowdy Christmas and New Year's Eve parties, Gilberto sat at a coffee shop near El Marqués, drinking coffee and listening to a giant radio tuned to a station playing boleros and news highlights. Analdo and he had agreed to meet early and take some groceries to Doña Sara's house, and he had arrived in time to order another hot coffee. There were a couple of businessmen there, and a bum or two looking for leftover food or cigarette butts on tables that had not been cleared yet. The brothers greeted each other and chatted. Analdo mentioned having seen Nélida looking the worse for wear and working in Los Nogales, a small makeshift bar outside Calarcá. He said she looked poorly because of a venereal disease that some client had given her, and according to those in the know, it was a bad bout. Gilberto felt very sad.

"Poor thing, my dear Nélida!" he reflected. He was concerned about her, for he had always considered her a good woman and an unconditional friend, the kind one rarely finds. He figured that the son he had possibly fathered with her must also be in trouble. Analdo told him that the little ones were doing well and were unaware of their mother's troubles because, according to Nélida, they had no idea of what was happening. She had told him that she had enrolled them in school, but because her husband had left her, she had been forced to go back to the brothels and had to pull them out of school. Gilberto pulled out a wad of bills, and, estimating, selected a few large ones and asked his brother to give them to her, so she could see a doctor and buy medicine. He also asked him to take some groceries that he would pack himself.

"Does María Sucel know about Nélida?" asked Analdo.

Surprised by the question, Gilberto replied in dismay, "How could you even ask that, for God's sake! She doesn't know about Nélida or anyone else. Anyway, poor Nélida doesn't worry me ... what terrifies me is my current situation." He proceeded to relate each of Ophir's recent appearances, and about the times that Ulises, her ex-husband, had challenged him outside of El Marqués, saying he knew that it was Gilberto's fault that she had left him.

After a few minutes with Analdo, and sick of talking about these thorny issues, he chose to talk about Cuba and its turmoil. His brother picked up the conversation, also aware of the situation on the island. He added that the rebels had forced Batista to run off. Eager to know how that was developing, Gilberto whistled for a newspaper vendor and bought the day's paper. He read the news out loud to Gilberto: "Batista, a Guest of Trujillo. Cuba is Free. Urgent Call to Castro. Country Celebrates the Fall of the Tyrannical Regime."

"The news from Cuba has piqued your interest," said Analdo. "Tell me exactly what happened. Things are really on fire!"

"That's right. What's happening is that this seems to be the latest trend, and I'm curious about how Batista's government let itself be ousted. The rebels have a very astute leader, someone called Fidel … Fidel Castro. But, let me read the details, because this is very interesting."

Analdo stooped to get a look at the San Francisco clock from under an eave. He reacted quickly and urged his brother to hurry up. Gilberto folded the newspaper and asked for their check, paying it promptly, and they headed to the warehouse. They ran into Don Aniceto, the bun vendor, at the corner. He greeted them warmly, and Gilberto took a couple of bags and asked him to put them on his account, to be paid at the end of the month. Arriving at El Marqués, he placed the paper bag on the ground to dig up the keys and unlock the padlocks. He switched some lights on as they entered, which helped illuminate the darkest corners of the warehouse as one of the cats approached to give them an affectionate, sleepy greeting. From his small office, he took an open bottle of milk and poured some in a bowl for the cat.

Analdo gathered some groceries for Nélida. Having been at the warehouse so often, he knew his way around quite well. Gilberto grabbed a stool from behind the counter and dragged it to the door, and tilting it, he balanced on the back legs and lit a cigarette. He concentrated on reading about Cuba as it dangled from his lips. The article said that numerous officials had fled with the dictator, and that a military junta led by General Cantillo had taken over. Breaking the silence, Gilberto read the last paragraph out loud: "Fidel Castro called on the people to trust no one, and not to let themselves be fooled." Satisfied by the good news, he folded the newspaper and stood up, walked to where Analdo was packing the groceries, and took the list. He took a pencil from his shirt pocket and added the bill up; then, in a notebook, he searched for the page where he kept a record of his personal accounts. These would be deducted from his salary, and he wrote down the total to be presented to Don Juvenal.

Several families depended on Gilberto, for aside from his own home with his wife —for which he was solely responsible— he helped with his parents Sara and Acasio's expenses, and even some of his sisters when they were in need. Furthermore, he contributed something to his in-laws out of his affection for them, though they had no need for help because Elías had savings that covered their expenses. Isabelina was a money-making machine, for she received a kind of payment from the fancier ladies, and even from the not-so-fancy ones. The payment was for praying novenas, so their husbands would be safe from lustful women and homewreckers, or trollops, as they called them when speaking among themselves. It seemed to Gilberto that he was assuming a new obligation from that day forward, to provide some type of monthly allowance for Nélida.

The day continued without much business, for El Marqués was as empty as La Galería generally. Only a few businesses were open, and Gilberto spent his time organizing some shelves. Around noon, the store guard brought in the lunch María Sucel had prepared for him, and he ate it right off the tray, being too lazy to serve it up on a plate. Seeing that there was little going on in the warehouse, Gilberto decided to lower the protective curtain, without locking up the store, and went into the office to do some paperwork. Outside the warehouse, while they waited to take their owners home or to one of the bars that were still open, horses ate from feedbags that had been hung around their necks to avoid making a mess on the street. Gilberto was surprised to hear the gate open and peeked through the window. Stepping out of the office, he was shocked to see Ophir. He stopped and nervously scratched his nose. She stood there looking at him, her face a picture of innocence.

"My God, woman! What are you doing here?"

"I came to wish you a Happy New Year …" she replied, shyly. "But, it's okay, sweetie. If you want me to leave, I'll go."

"I think that's good, Ophir! Just go to hell. Can't you see that you're driving me crazy?" he shouted, shaking her and pushing her towards the partially open gate. She wrenched herself free and shrank in fear, rubbing her sore arms. Seeing that Gilberto was serious, she sat down on a sack of beans, forlorn, and looked tiredly at him. Gilberto realized how rough he had been with her, a woman who had given him pleasure so many times within these very walls, the cats and some mice being their only witnesses. He was moved by her pain, and went to her then, hugging her gently and kissing her forehead.

"What are you two doing, getting into my life?" he complained. "You, trying to lure me all the time, and your husband coming over, who knows what the hell for. Weren't you separated? Stop trying to find me, Ophir, I beg you, for God's sake. Can't you see how I react?"

A shadow of fear and contradiction crossed Ophir's eyes, and she switched her submissive act to a much meaner one. The last thing she had expected was for her former lover to mention Ulises. Gilberto thought she was terrified of the guy; he had only seen him a few times in his life, but he could readily define him as a nasty, tyrannical, untrustworthy character. Deep down, he couldn't explain why Ophir had married him. María Sucel, at some point in her life, had told Tomás that Ulises had *bought* Ophir when she was very young. You would hear stories like that in those days. Something similar had even happened to Isabelina, with her first husband.

Ophir nervously stepped under the gate and scuttled away like a frightened snake. Remorse sank its teeth firmly into Gilberto, and he was overcome with doubts and conflicting emotions. He would have liked to make love to Ophir, because that girl was beautiful. However, he couldn't give in to such carnal feelings now, for current events in his life were becoming much too important. And on top of it all, his wife was pregnant again and almost ready to deliver.

As it neared El Paraíso, the rickety old rattletrap bus clattered in the cloud of dust created by its worn tires. This was an event that occurred every two hours in front of the Cervantes Barojas' house. When the bus approached, the dust followed it. But when it passed, that cloud of yellow dust mixed with the suffocating gray smoke that puffed out each time the driver, Don Nacianceno, shifted gears to pick up more speed. This was the best of the old carts covering the route from El Paraíso towards downtown and other parts of Armenia. The bus was named *El Cuyabro Consentido*, as stated on a sign painted in red; it had become the mechanical mascot of the town's young men, who hung on to its back fender and rode for a few blocks or as far as La Galería. Some people, supposedly those more refined, preferred to walk downtown rather than take the bus, which would mean putting up with gasoline smells filtering through the windows. Armenia was very small, and so it remained.

Never a day or night passed without that vehicle making its presence known in the neighborhood. It made such a loud racket that María Sucel and everyone in the whole sector could determine the time of day just by hearing the deafening noise of its tired but unfailing engine. When she heard it, to confirm the time when the bus would arrive bringing her husband home, she checked her Invicta brand wristwatch, which she always wore and which Gilberto had given her on the day Antonio was born. She would then increase the heat under the fried potatoes that would accompany beans for an early supper, which would be served before seven. The hungry man arrived promptly on the 6:25 bus, unless he was delayed by some infidelity with that old crone.

Across from María Sucel's house lived a family known for their quiet courteousness towards all their neighbors. The Cardonas were good friends with the Cervantes Barojas, especially the older generation: Doña Leticia and Don Arturo. The oldest daughter, Ruby, was the same age as María Sucel, and they got along so well she became her only friend and confidant. She was a gentle, humble girl, with great dignity, and like all the single women in El Paraíso, she spent her days immersed in the thankless drudgery of housework, which sometimes included polishing the wooden floors with steel wool, bringing them to a mirrorlike shine.

To the right of the Cardonas, also across from the Cervantes house, lived an inscrutable and not very sociable family of three: a burly, blond, blue-eyed man who worked for the Armenia fire department; his wife, Doña Inés, who took a confrontational attitude towards all her neighbors for no good reason, was skinny and gangly, had a nose like a witch, and never took off a black headband which she used to avoid combing her hair; and their daughter, a 20-year-old called Galilea, who kept to herself and had no friends. That house was the most disorganized in the neighborhood, in many unpleasant respects. It was unattractive, with its peeling paint, and it had an unkempt and dry garden. Their dog was the loudest in the area. This made them, of course, the subject of all the ladies' conversations, including María Sucel and Ruby, who never missed an opportunity to point out what horrible neighbors they were.

On the weekends, a group would gather at María Sucel's house to chat and play board games and cards: Don Arturo, Gilberto, Analdo, and older men like Elías and Acasio. They joked and drank glasses of aguardiente while listening to a professional soccer game, the sportscaster describing the successes and mistakes of their glorious local team, Atlético Quindío, which had recently won the championship. As usual, the women would serve their needs, interrupting occasionally. But they would chat amiably, sitting in front of the house, where there were always wicker chairs under an awning that provided shade when the sun shone brightly, letting them truly enjoy the temperate climate. Their conversation was restricted to predictable periods of time, because they never forgot that the old bus would arrive to ruin their clothes with its cloud of dust. Every time it happened, they would go inside the house to close the doors and windows, opening them again when the dust settled and allowed them at least another two hours of conversation. Towards the end of the 1950s, Armenia was still a prosperous and reputable place, and doors were left open during the day unless it rained. The few thieves that came around were chased away by the neighbors and subjected to lynching, shame, and jail, so civic solidarity was a widespread virtue.

sIn mid-September of 1959, María Sucel gave birth to another boy. They had prepared the layette in pink, in hopes of having a little girl. After sifting through many options, they agreed to call him Tomás, like Gilberto's brother-in-law, who was married to Romelia, his youngest sister and their mother's pet, whom they held in high regard.

A month after Tomás's birth, on one of his Tuesdays off, Gilberto rocked him to sleep in his arms, then took him to his bassinet and carefully put him down, covering him with kisses. The room where his wife rested was lit by a soft light; he partially opened the window, letting in a soft breeze that set the white, almost transparent curtains to waving. Leaving his slippers under the bed, he got under the sheets behind her, carefully, as if he might hurt her. He moved closer to feel her warmth and whispered in her ear that she should look through the window at the night sky.

She smiled with pleasure, turning to look into her husband's eyes. Before answering, she kissed him lovingly. "I see the stars; they glitter like my heart does when your body is so close to mine every night."

Gilberto held her in his arms and arranged the pillows so she could rest her head on his chest while looking at the sky, which was a deep blue in the moonlight. He stroked her hair, gently, endlessly, his deep voice leading her into a hypnotic trance. He murmured, "I have no words to tell you what I feel for you, but I know that it transcends time and space, that it is something so immense that it seems eternal. Never forget that."

Entranced, María Sucel grasped his strong arm and

quietly kissed his hands; they embraced tightly, each feeling that the other was the reason for their own existence.

In Paradise

...1961

Don Nacianceno always drove the old bus through El Paraíso, and sometimes a passenger he didn't know carefully observed the neighborhood. It was the third time that day that the excessively vain woman had ridden the bus. Intrigued, the driver kept his eyes on the rearview mirror, watching her constantly touch up her lipstick and smooth her eyebrows.

"Miss, are you looking for a particular place?" he finally asked courteously, during a stop to let off a passenger.

"Me?" the woman answered, pretending disinterest as she pointed to herself, with a certain snobbishness. "No, sir, I'm only familiarizing myself with the bus route. By the way, what neighborhood is this?"

"This is Corbones," replied Don Nacianceno, "and further ahead is El Paraíso, after we cross that park."

The brunette looked pleased and looked away from Don Nacianceno, who realized he should drive on without asking too many more questions. She asked to get off once they were in El Paraíso. Wordlessly, Don Nacianceno stopped the bus completely and waited a few seconds until the dust settled outside. Then he pushed the handle that opened the door. Some remnant dust entered the already dirty bus as the door opened. Standing on the street, the woman reluctantly shook the dust off her clothes and began to walk away slowly, looking around carefully. More than one neighbor noted the visitor's graceful and leisurely walk. The woman observed María Sucel's house for a minute; there was apparently nobody home. In moments, she noticed Doña Inés, the fireman's wife, opening wide the two sides of one of her windows.

"Are you looking for someone in El Paraíso?" she asked.

"No, ma'am, nobody specific. I'm just looking around the neighborhood. It's nice; I like it. I wouldn't mind living around here. It's just an idea I have. I live in a small room near La Galería," she explained. "I would like to be somewhere quieter, or at least not so loud. The noise of traffic and horses in downtown Armenia doesn't let me sleep."

"I see, I see," muttered Doña Inés, interested. "Do you live alone, or what?"

"Yes, my husband left me for another, and you know, things change."

"Well, don't just stand there, the sun is hot. Come over, have a drink of cool, clear maize. We keep it in a clay jug so it stays cold. My name is Inés, Inés de Ahumada."

"Pleased to meet you; my name is Ophir," she said, pretending embarrassment over Doña Inés's rare courtesy. It just goes to show that birds of a feather flock together. After Doña Inés insisted a few times, and they exchanged pleasantries, Ophir accepted the invitation. Asking about the neighbors, she learned that they had almost no contact with the Cardonas, who had a young daughter named Ruby. Their own daughter, Galilea, did not get along with Ruby, to the point of never exchanging a word or acknowledging each other. She learned that Galilea was a very quiet girl, an only child who helped with the housework and was submissive and obedient. Apparently, she was so reclusive she only left the house to go to mass on Sundays. Doña Inés also stated that Ruby was about twenty and quite friendly with a young woman from across the street called María Sucel de Cervantes, whom she labeled a homebody because she hardly ever even came to her window. Gossiping now, she announced that the woman had been pregnant since the day they moved into the neighborhood, and they already had two little boys. When asked about the husband, she declared that he seemed to be a serious man who was always home on Tuesdays. Based on appearances, the man even worked on Sundays, managing a large dry grocery in La Galería, where he was doing quite well, because their house was the prettiest in the neighborhood.

"I would really like to live around here. If you hear of any family who could rent me a room for a few days until my life returns to normal …"

Three days later, old Inés showed up at El Ruiz. Fortunately, though she had said she only worked there certain days, Ophir was working that day. She'd been working full time as an assistant since the day Gilberto offered to contact the owners of El Ruiz to ask them to hire her. Seeing her, Doña Inés quickened her pace and rushed to embrace her effusively. Ophir disentangled herself discreetly to avoid attention, and winked to warn her to remain circumspect at the workplace. Understanding, Inés acted cool, and began to run her hands through some beans in the sacks, as though comparing their quality.

"I bring good news," she announced. "We have a room available for you, in our home!"

Settled into the fireman's house, Ophir fell onto the soft mattress with its white purple-dotted sheets and took a deep breath. Her eyes focused on a point in the ceiling, glittering with nervousness and a touch of meanness. Her hands were trembling, her heart thumping so hard she thought it might leap out of her chest. As the day ended, most of the lights in the Ahumadas' house went out, and Ophir was possibly the only person in the neighborhood whose eyes remained open. Her mind was full of plans and fears. It was almost 2 a.m. when she turned off the light, and in the darkness, she walked to the window in the parlor, from which she admired Gilberto's home.

December came, and the families prepared to celebrate the Night of Little Candles to honor the Virgin Mary. María Sucel had gone downtown to shop with Ruby, while her mother babysat her two grandsons. People placed many colorful candles and dozens of paper lanterns in striking shades in front of their houses, so the neighbors could stroll along the streets and enjoy the December lights. Like the other husbands, Gilberto would bring fireworks when he arrived from work, especially sparklers and volcanoes. At six in the evening, María Sucel set colorful, long-tapered paraffin candles on the window ledges and the front yard, and lit them. Friends and acquaintances in El Paraíso were all doing the same, creating a picturesque, joyful spectacle of flickering lights. Gilberto arrived from work at eight o'clock and had a quick dinner, because El Paraíso was already all lit up, and they would also go out to join the celebration.

Fireworks lit up the sky in Quindío. All the townspeople were out on the streets, except for Ophir, who discreetly observed from her window as the Cervanteses chatted with Don Juvenal and the Cardonas. Ruby had joined the group and was very animated and friendly. The Ahumadas' house had only one white paper lantern hanging from the door frame, and the door remained open because of the celebration. Don Gabriel and Doña Inés chatted in the front room, while Galilea sat on the front stoop, enjoying the lights and listening to the laughter. It was difficult for her to join in the festivities; even more so because her parents kept to themselves. She sat in a poorly lit spot, sipping sweet wine that some neighbor had offered her, nibbling chocolate cookies with white cream in the middle.

"How about taking a walk around the neighborhood?" Doña Inés suggested, animated by the wine she'd already consumed. Ophir hadn't expected that, so she waited for Don Gabriel to respond.

"I think it's a good idea. It's an opportunity for Doña Ophir to meet more of our neighbors."

"You should go with Galilea, and I'll stay to watch the house."

"I think the four of us should go," insisted Don Gabriel. "It's not like we have any guests. This way, we can mingle and stretch our legs."

"Just give me a minute, please, to get ready," Ophir requested lightly. She bit her lip to keep her nerves at bay as she obsessively watched the Cervantes house. Her anonymity was undoubtedly about to disappear.

She returned a few minutes later, wearing a straight red dress that showed off her beautiful body. A tiny purse hung from her shoulder. Don Gabriel couldn't hide his admiration, though he pretended not to notice her. Ophir avoided looking at him; she knew she would make him uncomfortable, and it wasn't her intention to annoy Doña Inés. She stood near them without making eye contact; they were finally ready to leave. Doña Inés stepped out first, then Galilea, and then Ophir. Don Gabriel was the last one out, with the excuse of shutting the door, so he could enjoy the view of Ophir's backside—mentally undressing her with his eyes, as men often do when they look at women. María Sucel and Gilberto, Ruby and her parents Don Arturo and Doña Leticia, as well as Isabelina and Elías, were across the street. They chatted cheerfully, an open bottle of *aguardiente* nearby, as the radio played music in the background. Ruby held Antonio, the oldest, on her lap, and the grandmother held the youngest.

Ruby nodded discreetly towards María Sucel, murmuring, "Look who's coming from the fireman's house."

María Sucel took a quick look, and saw a woman walking saucily with the Ahumadas. "I wonder where that woman came from," María Sucel said. "It's strange to see the Ahumadas with anyone so striking."

"It's even stranger that the Ahumadas have come out to walk around the neighborhood today," added Ruby. She turned to Doña Leticia to alert her. "Mother, the Ahumadas are with someone we don't know."

Doña Leticia's face showed her consternation as she leaned forward to see. Intrigued, she continued her conversation with Don Arturo. María Sucel glanced at Gilberto, feeling for the first time a stab of jealousy as she sensed that the attractive stranger would surely catch his eye. She relaxed briefly when she saw him chatting with

Don Juvenal and Elías. Noticing how the woman invited her companions to walk in the middle of the street, María Sucel exchanged several knowing looks with Ruby. Isabelina also watched them smiling, except for Galilea, who followed the others, looking somber. Don Juvenal was the first of the men to notice the group. Seeing the Ahumadas out for a walk, he exclaimed sarcastically, "That's a first!"

Intrigued, Gilberto turned to see. Ophir's eyes pierced his senses. The whole world disappeared, and he didn't even hear the cacophonous booms of the fireworks. In an instant, everyone noted the red dress wrapping around the shapely legs, completely ignoring the insignificant purse on her shoulder. She had the men in a frenzy and the women upset, commenting among themselves. When he got himself back in control, Gilberto turned to look at his wife. Luckily for him, she was also watching the woman. He turned back to the group of neighbors and confirmed that it was indeed Ophir. Picking up his glass of *aguardiente*, he downed it in one gulp.

"That woman looks a lot like Ophir. Do you think it's her?" Don Juvenal whispered to Gilberto. Feeling trapped, Gilberto told him to keep quiet. Don Juvenal looked at María Sucel, who had noticed that they were whispering secretively, and smiled at her uncomfortably. Meanwhile, Gilberto offered Elías more *aguardiente* to avoid looking at his wife. She realized they were talking about the woman and decided not to consider it strange. The Ahumadas walked by, looking elsewhere to avoid greeting them, but Ophir approached them with a smile.

"Good evening!"

"Good evening," they replied together.

The perverse woman didn't look at anyone in

particular; she knew that Gilberto had recognized her, and that was enough. She continued walking, leaving Gilberto livid about having been put in a compromising situation.

María Sucel, noticing he seemed tense and uncomfortable, asked, "Dear, are you feeling well? You're pale. Is the *aguardiente* upsetting your stomach?" He shook his head, not knowing what to answer, then told her he had a bit of indigestion and needed to step away to the bathroom for a moment.

Isabelina was thoughtful, for Ophir's face was familiar to her. Shuffling through her memories, she recalled someone similar who had admired the embroidery she had helped her daughter prepare for her mother-in-law. Turning to Elías, she asked if that girl had looked familiar to him. Elías had also thought she looked like the girl from El Marqués, remembering when she had helped Gilberto wrap the embroidery for Doña Sara. But they decided it couldn't be the same person, for otherwise Gilberto would certainly have greeted her, and so would Don Juvenal.

Though at the age of sixty-eight his soul was at ease, Elías's drooping eyelids made his face look tired. He was retired now, but kept busy with a woodworking hobby and making toys for his grandchildren. Isabelina made them cloth dolls using fabric remnants and pieces of old nylon stockings. Today, she was making a doll for Piedad, María Sucel's youngest daughter, who had been born in July 1961. She now had three children.

"Dear, some coffee to quench this thirst would be really nice, don't you think?" Elías suggested cheekily. Isabelina continued stitching and didn't answer. Her husband didn't insist; he knew she had heard him and would get up from her rocking chair in a minute to go to the kitchen for coffee.

They sat and recalled past concerns over their daughter's love life, and smiled as they wistfully acknowledged how difficult those days had been. On the outside, they had taken Ophir's strange presence in El Paraíso calmly. Elías said he had seen her working in La Galería at a dry grocer's called El Ruiz. They thought it strange that she was living so close by but agreed to stop speculating about it and avoid potential embarrassment. But they also decided to make sure it was the same girl who had worked with their son-in-law at El Marqués years earlier. Neither could explain why, on the Night of the Candles, she had walked by pretending she didn't know any of them, and neither Gilberto nor Don Juvenal had said a word.

Elías put his tools away neatly to continue working the following day, rinsed his face with water from a pitcher near the sink, and then dried himself with a cloth that always hung there.

"I have a hankering, and I'm going to La Galería for some buns," he told his wife. "But I'll take the bus, because I'm quite tired." Elías left the house and started walking, hoping that the bus would come by at some point. He got on it in Corbones, about five minutes after leaving El Paraíso. He sat next to the driver, and he and Don Nacianceno chatted like cronies. They talked about the newly paved road, and how the neighbors could now keep their homes free of the ubiquitous dust. In his youth, Elías had supervised road work; he was pleased with the city's progress and, since he was sitting in a good spot, proudly brought up the subject with the driver.

"Did you know that we laid down the roads across Caldas in 1939? Those were wonderful years. I had many responsibilities. I supervised over one hundred workers, from one town to the next, pouring concrete on the roads."

"Well, Don Elías, you men did a great job. I've always wondered how they could pave so many roads in those steep mountains."

"It wasn't easy! Let me give you the quick version: my son-in-law Eliseo, who is now married to my oldest daughter, dynamited the rocks with precision, one kilometer ahead of our crews. We leveled and flattened the dirt, and placed the forms that we later filled with cement. Those were hot days and physically very exhausting, but there's no doubt that, for me, those were the best of times."

Time flew as they talked. Arriving at La Galería, Elías searched out Don Aniceto and bought a bag of buns. He pulled from his pocket a mesh bag woven from fine agave cord, which he always brought along to carry his purchases.

He walked slowly, mingling with the people, until he located El Ruiz, where he stood for a few minutes, unobserved. Trying to see, unsure of how much he wanted to see, he noticed Ophir come in from some other section, smiling and humming. Men stared fixedly as she sashayed by, her tightly covered buttocks swaying as if to a beat. Elías was sure now that this was the same woman that he and Isabelina had been talking about. He crossed the street to one of the coffee shops and watched while sipping an unsweetened cappuccino. After a few minutes, the metallic curtains clanged noisily as they closed, announcing the exit of storekeepers and the arrival of garbage men and other people who inhabit the night. The coffee shops acquired a different atmosphere with the arrival of the bar girls; as darkness fell, they became gentlemen's entertainment centers. Elías kept a newspaper open in front of his face to discourage the waitress; to extend his stay, he ordered another cappuccino, which she brought promptly. He watched Ophir leave the dry grocer's, striding along as she looked at herself vainly in a small mirror, arranging her hair and touching up her lipstick, all the while swinging her hips rhythmically. Elías left the coffee shop and followed her. Pausing on the corner opposite La Galería, she stood there a minute, still looking at her compact. Some men walking by turned their heads to take her in; some even murmured suggestively. Ophir ignored them, acting as if she didn't want attention, something her attractive figure made impossible. This continued uneventfully, until Elías noticed Gilberto walking in front of El Ruiz, peering inside without stopping. He bought some buns from Don Aniceto, then walked towards the corner where Ophir was still standing. They walked along at some distance from one another, but his father-in-law clearly understood that they were going somewhere together. The younger man caught up with Ophir, occasionally glancing around; they walked a couple of blocks farther. The woman unexpectedly quickened her pace and magically disappeared through the door of a three-story building. Gilberto paused, evidently making sure nobody was watching, and then also entered the building a few seconds later.

Taken aback by what he had seen, Elías thought in a flash of María Sucel and felt faint. He approached the building, verified that the couple was not standing in the lobby, and went inside. A woman approached and cordially asked him, "Are you waiting for someone, or would you like to meet the escort ladies here?" Confused by this, without looking at her or answering, Elías turned and left. He now had a secret he would never reveal, not even to his wife. He walked, and walked, and walked, downcast and crushed.

Visiting La Galería every Friday evening in the course of several months, old Elías obtained undeniable proof. Although Isabelina tried to get to the bottom of his sour mood, he never told her about their son-in-law's erotic adventures.

By June 1963, the Cervantes Baroja family numbered six, Maru having arrived the previous September. She was a bright little girl with big, expressive black eyes, who at nine months charmed everyone with her antics. That Tuesday, Gilberto was resting when Isabelina arrived at the house wearing a medium-sized mantle, a sad look on her face. She announced that she would be late coming back from church, because Pope John XXIII had given up his soul to the Lord the night before. Since it was about His Holiness, María Sucel decided to accompany her. Elías arrived a few minutes later, and, referring to the Pope's death, stated that everyone had to die, and should die without remorse and at peace with God and with others. A couple of chickens pecked at the packed dirt on the patio; Muñeca, the old dog, scared them off and made them cackle. A cool breeze rose from the canyon; the solitude was pleasing.

"We've seen three popes die in the course of our lives, or I should say, in the course of my life. I don't know if you've seen more of them die in your lifetime," said Gilberto.

"I can only remember three, I think, but this one left quickly," replied Elías, and sipped his hot coffee. He lit a cigarette, offering his son-in-law one as well. The smoke was a participant in the conversation, hovering between Gilberto's slow movements and Elías's disturbing truth.

"You're over forty years old now, and you must know that my daughter's love for you is the purest kind," the elder man said. "Ever since María Sucel first received your flowers, as a mere child, she thought they were the most sublime in the world, and that they represented only love. What she is unaware of is that they are a disguise, a farce, a pretense of love held up by appearances. Each petal you give her carries a message that numbs her and impedes her thinking, not letting her understand the truth about life. While the flowers arrive, her children are born, and while her children are born, you have appointments a few blocks away from El Marqués, every Friday, with the neighbor from across the street."

Gilberto paled, his eyes widening at what he heard; his lips were white, his hands pulled at his hair in despair. He dared not look at the older man. He took a deep breath and exhaled, feeling miserable and lost. He was a cheat and unable to deny it, for Elías was such a respectable man that it would be shameful to even try to dissuade him.

"You should know, *Don Gilberto*," he sneered, "that for several months I've watched you going into the rooming house with Ophir, the one from El Ruiz; the neighbor from across the street from María Sucel's house. The very one I recognized that December on the Night of Candles, strutting around the neighborhood in a lovely, bewitching red dress; the one who greeted us. You knew it was her, but you pretended you didn't know her, like the asshole you are. Both you and Don Juvenal kept quiet. I remembered that she was the one who showered with compliments the embroidery that you asked my daughter to make for your mother. But I've kept quiet, only because of the love I have for my family. The best thing is that María Sucel doesn't know, and lucky for you, she doesn't suspect, either."

Gilberto realized that his life was exactly as it had been when he was twenty and Doña Sara had kicked him out. Despite having been found out by his father-in-law, he thanked God that it was still a secret between the two of them, and his wife was unaware of his shameless behavior. After ten or fifteen minutes, old Elías left the house without turning around, or even glancing at him.

María Sucel became pregnant again, and her vase always had an arrangement of fresh flowers that arrived every Monday.

Ofir... Ofir...

...1964

Their ears attuned to the radio, Analdo, Acasio, and Gilberto listened excitedly to a tight finish at the Sunday races.

"... On the riiiight ... Aladdin is head-to-head with Aguardiente. Gaining two lengths, it's Bambuco approaching on the left flank, very strong, he's starting to shorten the distance, now he's only one length away from Aladdin ... Aguardiente begins to fall behind and Aladdin holds, but it's difficult ... Serrano is barreling in on the left, with only one hundred meters to the finish line ... This will be a photo finish; there are now three horses holding steady in the lead! Serrano is giving it a devil's push, and is starting to take the lead ... and it's Serrano in first place, Aladdin coming in second, Aguardiente is third ..."

Gilberto, holding the transistor radio in his hand, sprung up from his chair. "Daaaamnnn! I almost won! If that Serrano hadn't come in so strong at the end, I would have won some money ..."

Laughing at one another, frustrated, swearing left and right, they tore up their betting slips. The Cervantes family bet on the horses every weekend, and part of the ritual was to listen to the races, and to professional soccer games, on the radio. It had become a family tradition that brought them all together around the paternal grandparents, who lived in a large house in the Granada neighborhood with their two unmarried children: Federica, called La Ñata because a rare childhood disease had deformed her nose, and pampered Sigifredo. At thirty-two, his parents still supported him, and his devoted mother pampered him. He was the best-known cardsharp in the brothels of Armenia, where he spent his time playing pool and poker. Years later, when his speech was unintelligible and he was permanently palsied after getting a severe beating at some point, he could be found wandering around Bogotá's drug slums. Nobody knows anything about his fate for certain, but stories are told.

Although these Sunday gatherings almost always took place at the home of the paternal grandparents, that Sunday, Gilberto had kindly invited everyone to his home since María Sucel was still recovering after giving birth, for the fifth time in barely six years. Named Sarita, after her grandmother, the girl had arrived only nine days previous, on February 8th. The entire family had attended.

On the Baroja side, only grandmother Isabelina was present. As she did after every other birth, she diligently took care of her daughter and took over the domestic chores. The gathering was full of kindness, for Dora, as well as Romelia and Martha, Uncle Analdo's wife, helped Isabelina with the food, while the men entertained the little ones with games.

They were almost all gathered around María Sucel's bed, laughing at foolishness from Analdo and Gilberto, who were unrecognizable that day. They were usually quite serious people, not given to joking. María, meanwhile, nursed Sarita, having discreetly covered herself with a square of hemmed flannel. It was a complicated situation, because little Maru kept pulling on the sleeve of her nightgown, wanting her turn at her mother's breast. After six years, María Sucel had become a nursing professional, alternating between her babies. Gilberto distracted Maru so she wouldn't pester her mother.

"We've never lacked for work and sustenance, or love," boasted Gilberto. "I'd venture to say that now we need another little boy, to balance the family," he added. "I actually think that we're at a disadvantage now, because there are more women than men in this house, and that's just not right." Everyone laughed at this.

María Sucel looked at him sharply, yet mischievously, feeling a bit pampered. "You'll have to give birth to him yourself, dear, because I'm about to burst from feeding little ones," she stated, practically confessing her true feelings.

Everyone present expressed disapproval at that, especially grandmother Sara, who felt that it was God's gift to have numerous children. Gilberto became affectionate and covered María Sucel with kisses until she blushed.

Despite the confrontation with Elías, Gilberto continued supporting Ophir in her apartment near La Galería. He quite frequently visited her there clandestinely, despite knowing of Ulises' secret assaults. She had beseeched him to stay calm and avoid all contact with the man, and never to confront him, because he was prone to violence and often carried a gun. He heeded his lover, who probably knew there was a reason to be afraid. For Gilberto, Ulises was a difficult character to accept, a piece of shit, and this stuck in his craw.

Their secret arrangement would never change. They were both quite sure that Gilberto's clandestine visits to Ophir would continue, since he had ordered her to quit El Ruiz to avoid Elías's watchful eye. Unable to stomach his hypocrisy, the old man had stopped visiting María Sucel, blaming his excessive cough or saying he suffered from age-related ailments like headaches. She made sure to visit him whenever she could, always ensuring he spent special time with his grandchildren.

Although she no longer lived in El Paraíso, Ophir, using tricks she had used when she lived with the Ahumadas, managed to wangle her way into María Sucel's home. She would bring over a little "something" to share at tea time, for example. Inevitably, this new form of blackmail that Ophir had instigated under his nose and without his knowledge increasingly stressed Gilberto. He knew that what he was doing wasn't right, but that woman had him "pussy-whipped," or bewitched, or something. She had started to milk him for money under the pretext of holding it as a safety net, so that even if they had to keep it hidden, their relationship wouldn't end from one day to the next. The thing is, the situation overwhelmed Gilberto. The novelty of secret meetings with her had become a strange kind of habit, though by then they had been at it for fifteen years. Besides, those encounters intensified during the months when my mother was pregnant. My father had ceded the management of several of his savings accounts to Ophir, since she had helped him with bookkeeping during her time at El Marqués, and, though she informed him of how much she took for groceries, he never asked to see the accounting.

The day before the celebration of the discovery of the Americas, in October 1965, the Cervantes family was invited to a farm located in Montenegro, not too far from Armenia. Generously, Gilberto had asked a select group of his wife's friends to come, so they could help with the children, especially because she was again about to give birth. Her friend Ruby and Doña Leticia, her mother, were both invited, together with Isabelina, and even Berenice, the new midwife, who was closely monitoring the pregnancy, now in its eighth month. Two days before that family outing, Ophir showed up at María Sucel's house with a big smile and a package, wrapped in pink paper with harlequins printed on it.

"And how is the pregnant lady of the house?" she greeted her cheerfully.

"Very well, thank you. You shouldn't have bothered …"

"It's just a small token of affection," Ophir assured her, wishing her well. They went into the parlor and, without having been offered a seat, Ophir settled herself on the sofa while she admired the house. Ingratiatingly, she implied that Gilberto surely enjoyed having his house always so neat and inviting. María Sucel replied that even when she was single, she had always been neat, and thanked her for the baby booties. Timid in Ophir's presence but excited over a new visitor, Piedad, one of the younger daughters, approached. The blondest of the children, at age four she had enough energy to play with and distract precocious little Maru. Fortunately for María Sucel, both Antonio and her second son went to first grade until noon. Since this was an unexpected visit, she had no choice but to receive her guest in the kitchen, where she was in the middle of peeling and chopping vegetables and preparing other ingredients for the midday meal.

"I'm so sorry to bother you so early. Is there anything I can help you with?" exclaimed Ophir, acting considerate.

"Don't worry. Sit here on this bench while I finish seasoning my stew. Tell me, how are you getting on at El Ruiz?"

"I don't work there anymore, because the man I live with doesn't like me to be in the company of so many men.

As if their stares would leave me less attractive to him. You know how jealous men are. It's best not to give them any reasons."

"I didn't know you had someone permanent with you."

"That's right. I have a very dear and special man, though he has a private life."

"And ... how long have you been together?" asked María Sucel.

"Oh, dear, who can remember? If I tell you, you'll fall flat on your back, and with that big belly ..."

"That bad?"

"We've known each other for fifteen years. We've spent some time apart, but have always gotten back together again."

"Who is he?"

"It's a man who works in La Galería, in one of the dry grocer's."

"Then, Gilberto must know him, especially if he's been there so many years," María Sucel suggested.

"I'm sure he does. La Galería is a small place, everyone always sniffing after everyone's business. Yes ... they're acquaintances, because they've always had contact through their work. Well, they haven't spent time lately because each one is busy with their own things. Whatever, El Ruiz and El Marqués are always fighting over the best customers, and that keeps them apart a bit. I think Don Gilberto might not know we're a couple. Well ... I wouldn't say he's my husband, because the fact that he's paying for the apartment doesn't mean there's anything more involved than being together. It's more like he is my man."

"I see ... Have you thought of getting married?"

"I wish, but he's already married and has a lot of

kids," explained Ophir.

"And you enjoy that? Are you resigned to it?"

"Never! Like a fool, I promised to keep quiet. It was his only condition for us to be together. He takes care of my passions and tries hard to be very special. I don't have to worry about my food, my clothes, or shoes. The ones who should worry are his wife and children. Things are very clear; he trusts me, so much that I even help him with his accounts. It's ironic. Sometimes he asks me about money for things for his wife and children. The thing is that I know a lot about bookkeeping, and he likes that."

"I think I'm a little nervous," María Sucel confessed. "I think about Gilberto and can't help comparing him to all the men who need to have secret affairs."

"Have you ever been jealous of your husband?" asked Ophir.

"I never have. But, if I think about it, maybe that's not true. Only once did I feel jealous. When he met you that December, on the Day of Candles. Do you remember? You had recently arrived in El Paraíso and were walking through the neighborhood with the Ahumadas."

"But, what an idea!" Ophir laughed. "How could you be jealous of me? I'm your friend. How did you get rid of those feelings of jealousy?"

"Quite easily," she answered sincerely. "I asked him why he was looking at you so much, and he told me."

"This truly is funny. And what was the reason, if you don't mind telling me?" asked Ophir, laughing again as she pretended to be hearing something outrageous.

"Forgive me. I didn't mean to be so thoughtless, sharing intimacies like that. Just for your peace of mind, I'll tell you that he said that he thought you looked familiar, and now I think that must have been true. Perhaps he had seen you in La Galería," María Sucel explained. "Gilberto said that he loved only me, and that was enough for me. You don't think he'd have given me so many children if he didn't love me!" she added.

As they continued chatting, Ophir learned about the outing to the farm and immediately expressed her desire to come with them.

When Gilberto arrived, as usual, Antonio and Tomás proudly showed him the work they had done at school that day. Gilberto gave them candy and picked Maru up. María Sucel welcomed him cheerfully, and he caressed her stomach, which was carrying Cesarino. Then he sat on one of the little benches next to the table where Piedad and Sara were eating. The children laughed at his discomfort but enjoyed playing with him and taking advantage of all the possibilities offered by his loving presence. Disheveled from their attention, his eyes never left María Sucel as he attempted to talk in the middle of the children's antics.

"How was everything around here?" asked Gilberto.

"Fine. I had the strangest visitor, or I should say, an unexpected visitor."

"Who was it, dear?" he wondered.

"Ophir, the one who lived across the street … in the fireman's house."

"What did that woman come here for?" he demanded indignantly, pressing his lips together. María Sucel walked to the parlor and returned with the booties, still in their wrapping paper. Gently, she put them on the table and went back to her frying pan to finish preparing dinner. Gilberto couldn't get over his lover's nerve. He needed more details.

"What does this mean?"

"She said she wanted to give me something for the new baby. Don't you think they're cute?"

"Yes, they are. How long did she stay?"

"Not much, just half an hour. She played a lot with Sarita and chatted with me while I did my chores. It's ironic. The poor thing hasn't been able to have children; she misses that. That's why she brought the gift. According to what she said, she likes to celebrate other people's children. She even said she'd like to come with us to the farm; asked me about it when she heard we were going. She offered to look after Sarita. From what I could see, she was very taken with her."

"And what did you tell her?" he asked, concerned.

"I tried to dissuade her because she was so insistent. She even said she was going to be alone because her boyfriend, or her man, couldn't be with her that day."

Gilberto's conscience hit him fiercely. He knew he was being unfair and a hypocrite. The happiness he was enjoying, with his children crawling over him, and his pregnant wife, all seemed fictitious. He was a wretch.

María Sucel continued analyzing the situation while she set the table in the improvised dining room. "You know, dear, we don't know much about Ophir. She mentioned that her boyfriend was a married man, someone from La Galería, and said that you probably knew him. She seems a bit enigmatic. And she's not ugly, you know? She has a very nice shape, and her face is very attractive."

"I know little about the woman," he replied, upset. "I've seen her, I can't deny it. I know the people at El Ruiz; we just cross paths and say hello now and again. We've never even had coffee together." He tickled Antonio to avoid the subject, and fortunately, the child laughed excitedly. Gilberto was quiet then, his eyes fixed on the hot food.

He pulled the sheet off her curvy body angrily, uncovering her. He opened the curtains, letting light in; when the sun shone on her sleeping face, Ophir blinked like a bat. Gilberto's mood scared her, he was so upset, but she pretended to be calm as he sat hunched over on the edge of the bed. Gilberto demanded she never go to his home again. Wordlessly, she curled up in an intimidated fetal position. Then she got up and covered her nudity with a robe, and slowly went to the kitchen, ignoring her lover. Following her, Gilberto watched her filtering the coffee, her head down and her eyes full of tears. She held the tiny cup of coffee between her hands and walked back to the bedroom. Leaving the cup on the bedside table, she went to the window that Gilberto had opened and closed the curtains, plunging the room into darkness. Getting into bed, she placed the pillow behind her back, covered her legs with the sheet, and sipped her coffee carefully so as not to burn her lips. Ophir wept, but not a sound left her throat. Moved, he returned to the room and sat on the bed. He lit a cigarette and smoked it down completely.

"We cannot set aside our promise of silence," said Gilberto, calmer now. "We are lovers, and that's that."

Ophir continued weeping, her eyes fixed on the drop of coffee remaining in the cup. She felt miserable and misunderstood. She felt that their breakup was imminent, that the agony of unresolved issues could no longer be put off, and she turned to him in despair. "Does that mean that for your world to turn smoothly, I'm the only one who must leave? Where do I put all those years that I've spent waiting for you to love me?"

"In your conscience," he replied, "in the deepest part of yourself. I'll do the same. I'll leave without you and remember you with affection. You're young and beautiful, and deserve to find true love outside of El Marqués."

Incredulous, her mouth busy with pins she was using to put up her hair, Ophir looked at him. "Give me time, a few months, a few years, to get used to the idea that I won't die over this. Stop coming over so often. Visit only once a month until I don't need to see you. Someday you'll come, and I won't be waiting for you anymore."

Overwhelmed, Gilberto returned to El Marqués, where many people were demanding his attention. At sunset, feeling pressed to find solutions, he decided to take a walk. He climbed the steps to San Francisco church and crossed himself. At the door, he asked God for illumination. Half kneeling, he crossed himself again and walked on despondently, smoking a cigarette. To ease his confusion, he loosened the knot in his tie and rolled up his shirt cuffs. His thoughts bounced between his wife, his lover and the sinister character of Ulises, and between the truth that Elías knew and his children's faces. The hope of the child on the way contrasted with his disappointment over the breakup. Never far from his thoughts was the unwavering Nélida, and even his possible son. He thought about other possible sons and daughters he had never met. Such was his despair that he was beginning to seek radical solutions. It was essential to put a stop to Ophir's harassment, but it wasn't enough to say goodbye and leave her. She had to physically disappear, at the very least. But, how could he banish his dear Ophir and ignore all her expectations? There were no easy answers.

His steps took his sorry self to the park where he had taken refuge when Elías had caught him in his infidelity. Where the stone nymph reminded him of his wife and her slender figure. Where lovers played at hitting lily pads with tiny stones, with an openness that he envied.

Cesarino's birth renewed the Cervantes Barojas' verve. The radio once again played loudly, delighting everyone, and history repeated itself with new characters taking part in the celebrations. Family and friends gathered, even those arriving from Manizales, and other old neighbors who came to honor the prettiest baby in the entire neighborhood. It was an unforgettable feast, celebrated on Saturday, February 19, 1966. Surely never before had any family organized a noisier party in El Paraíso, nor one as well-attended. Not even the Arará family, which was very rambunctious because they were from the Atlantic coast. The festivities lasted until dawn, and many happy drunks ended up drinking *aguardiente* in the middle of the street, arguing and passionately defending the political merits of the presidential candidates who would face one another for the presidency the following May. Gilberto himself, discombobulated by drink, his eyes half closed, attempted to explain to Analdo his political affinity amid a common enthusiasm for the party in those days, prior to the most important elections in recent history. Hazy and uncoordinated, Gilberto was giving a speech, his words interrupted by hiccups, burps, and interspersed with spitting.

"I may be an inveterate conservative, like my father before me, but I defend my position in favor of Carlos Lleras Restrepo! Little do I care if he's a liberal. Any self-respecting, well-born conservative must vote for the man!"

Something Other Than a Prayer

...1968

Seeing that it wasn't Iphigenia at the door, María Sucel went to see to whom Rosalía was speaking. She took over and greeted the stranger; it was a woman asking for Don Gilberto. She thought it might be one of those women requesting a prayer and asked her to try again later, explaining that he could only see her after three in the afternoon. The woman thanked her and clearly stated that she would stand outside the house until he got home, because, she said, she couldn't let him slip away. Bewildered, María Sucel asked if there was anything she could do until her husband arrived.

"Did you say your husband?" asked the woman.

"Yes, my husband, Don Gilberto, the one you're here to see." The woman looked confused and then tried to clear it up by describing Gilberto as a man with curly hair and gray eyes, who always dressed in a dark suit. María Sucel confirmed it was him but still didn't understand what the problem was. Even Rosalía was confused by the questions and incoherent answers. The three women stood at the street door, perplexed. The stranger asked to speak with her for a minute to untangle this strange situation, and María Sucel invited her to come in.

"Come in, please, come in," she invited, apologizing for the mess. "I wasn't expecting visitors this early." The woman came inside, looking around for answers. She saw the children playing in the bedroom, filling the home with their happy noise. She also noticed all the beds placed geometrically, occupying almost all the available space, but was pleased to see everything clean and looking neat. María Sucel offered her something to drink and asked her to sit on one of the beds that had already been made. The woman turned down the offer for a drink but sat down and asked if they could speak privately. Rosalía took the children outside.

"You are Don Gilberto's wife, and these are your children? This is your home?" the woman asked once again, seeing the wedding photo hanging on the wall, next to the Sacred Heart of Jesus. María Sucel nodded, looking at her without saying a word. The next question was very strange.

"Do you know someone named Ophir?"

"Yes, of course. I know her."

The woman gently took hold of María Sucel's hands, to help her understand. She explained that she had thought Ophir was Don Gilberto's wife. María Sucel smiled openly, thinking that she was misinformed, but the woman denied this, frowning with regret. She said that for several months, Gilberto had been living with Ophir in an apartment that she rented to them, on the south side of Bogotá. He had told her himself that they had been married in Armenia many years earlier, and that he worked over in Villavicencio, so he was often not at home. The woman announced that, having had a very difficult time conceiving, Ophir was finally pregnant at forty-two, about five months along now. Lastly, she said that the reason she had been standing in front of the house was because she was tracking Gilberto to force him to pay the three months' rent he owed, plus other loans for shopping.

María Sucel couldn't bear it. She covered her face with her bony hands. What she had just heard devastated her soul; shocked, she couldn't react. The pain was so deep that it settled into her heart, barely revealed on her face. For a few seconds, she thought that maybe it was just a dream, one she would wake up from at any moment. But as she lowered her hands, she saw before her the woman who had brought this horrible story, and she began to believe her.

"Are you sure of what you're telling me, ma'am?" María Sucel hurried to the cabinet and pulled an album from one of the compartments. She had filled it with photos from the past, a testimony to many joys and misadventures. She opened it to a page with a photo showing herself standing next to Gilberto, surrounded by the children in the park, the same park where he had gone to reflect on his adultery after being discovered by Elías. She was hoping the face wasn't the one the stranger remembered, but it was no use. The woman confirmed it.

María Sucel refused to cry. Bitterly, like a criminal surrendering to authorities, she told the woman that her husband would be home around two, and asked her to come at that time to ask him for the money. Meanwhile, she would think about what she would do. Suggesting the woman should go have some coffee while she waited, she directed her to Don Alirio's bakery. Then María Sucel took refuge in the bathroom and locked the door. Weeping inconsolably, she ignored Rosalía's pleas to open the door. Only minutes passed, but they seemed like hours. At last she gave Rosalía a brief explanation of what she had just learned, then went to kiss each of her children, while praying about their futures.

She went to Doña Iphigenia's house and waited there, for she didn't want to witness Gilberto's arrival or hear that woman's demands. She didn't want to see her beloved husband's sorry face. The husband who had flooded her with weekly flowers until she fell madly in love at the dawn of her life. The one she'd dutifully blessed with so many children, to whom she'd sworn fidelity until death. She thought about all of Ophir's appearances in the past, as mysterious as they were untimely, and his brazen betrayal while she was raising their children hurt even more. She remembered that her father, Elías, had wisely, firmly, opposed the relationship from the beginning. She thought of people who must have been aware of the situation but pretended to be ignorant of it—like Analdo, whom she now considered a Judas, and his buddy, Don Juvenal—and hated them all. She had no doubt that they all knew perfectly well about that woman. María Sucel condemned the way Gilberto, a few months earlier, had dared to bring his lover into their home, allowed her to sleep in their own bed—both women pregnant at the time. Cursing her children's father as a shameless imbecile, she wept. She cried whenever the good times they had known crept into her mind; she cried remembering her wedding day. She cried as she relived each of her eight deliveries. She cried when she recalled leaving her land, and that first terrible night when they had arrived in Bogotá. She abhorred Ophir's hypocrisy of friendship, and understood now her discreet presence outside their house in El Paraíso, and that time she had asked to accompany them on their picnic. She understood why Ophir had always been an undecipherable shadow, an unknown presence wandering through their lives, clad in a diaphanous mantle of friendship and affection. She cried and cried.

Unaware of the whole situation, Gilberto cheerfully arrived home on time. Rosalía decided to warn him, and after he finished putting away the iron cart in the patio, she nervously told him all of it. The man reclined against the wall and slid down until he was sitting on the freezing concrete. Pulling up his legs, he lowered his head onto his knees and covered his ears. Pale and shocked, he rubbed his mouth and then his eyes, leaving them reddened. He sat there, looking everywhere, without saying a word, until they heard the knocking on the gate that announced the unavoidable two o'clock appointment. Gritting his teeth, he moaned in frustration.

"Are you going to open the door, or do you want me to do it?" asked Rosalía.

Not knowing what to say, he looked at the sky, furious, but its grayness offered no clarity. The knocking continued. He stood up in exasperation and went to open the door, telling Rosalía to keep the children distracted so they wouldn't see anything they shouldn't. As he opened the door, the woman, forgoing a greeting, told him firmly that she would not budge from his doorstep until he paid her what he owed. Embarrassed, Gilberto stared at her, acutely aware once again that he was failing. he'd failed Doña Sara years earlier, he'd failed his wife, and who knows how many others he'd failed. He didn't reproach her for having come to María Sucel's house to find him, because his actions left him no moral grounds to do so. He opted for taking some cash out of his pocket. Turning his back, he counted out the right amount, then handed it over and apologized to the woman before she left.

When not a soul could be seen on the streets of La Granja, Gilberto finally stumbled home under the effects of the alcohol running through his veins. At that hour, one was supposed to walk confidently, sober, vigilant, to avoid being mugged; but he had faith in the saying that God looks out for drunkards. Meanwhile, María Sucel had decided that he would never see traces of her tears, although her eyes were swollen from crying so much. When he opened both locks in the iron gate and entered the small brick hallway that led to the patio, Gilberto felt that, even in his own home, darkness was his only friend. Walking across the small patio, he felt chilled by a terrible loneliness, and he shivered. In the midst of his inebriated haze, he was aware that every member of that household was suffering the consequences of his actions. In the bathroom, he turned on the light and urinated, splashing the bowl, and mopped it up poorly with toilet paper. Rinsing his hands in the sink, he purposefully made noise, seeking to rouse some indication of movement or voices that might comfort him, to no avail. His bumbling alerted no one. He expected María Sucel to come out at any moment, shouting, demanding, insulting him, but that didn't happen either. Her silence was eloquent.

After smoking two cigarettes, he decided to open the door to the bedroom, which was completely dark and where nothing moved. The warmth inside his home was a contrast to the patio's chill, but it couldn't take the sorrowful chill from his guts. Approaching his marriage bed, he found it empty, and understood then that, as it had been desecrated, he would sleep there alone. He searched hard for María Sucel's shape somewhere in the darkness, panicking to think he might have been left without her. He turned the covers back on each sleeping body, searching erratically, increasingly crazed, and sighed with relief when he found her sleeping comfortably in one of the smaller beds with two of the children. Finally grasping the meaning of this wordless image, he felt the strength of her rejection. Sensing his wife was merely pretending to sleep, he stayed there, in the shadows, feeling the emptiness of her presence. In his wife's silent detachment, the loss of her unconditional friendship, he envisioned the intense drama of seeing everything he'd done over thirty years collapse. Beginning with María Sucel's baby babbles, which had so captivated him in Salamina, until the moments in the metal bed when they conceived their family and spent hours talking happily, unforgettably.

Meanwhile, María Sucel clung to the warmth of Juan de Dios and Maru. Her eyes closed, she was awake and expectant, pretending to sleep. Though she wanted to explode, after thinking about it all day long, she had decided not to. Time would take care of calming her anger until reason could prevail. In the following days, all the love she felt for her children flowed from María Sucel's every pore, but she never even glanced at Gilberto, who wandered about, defeated and drunk.

Several days later, mourners stood to the left of the priest, while the funeral home employees rested before carrying the coffin to the grave, as everyone watched. Don Acasio had died when his lungs gave up, the first of the Cervantes clan to leave this earth. Someone had clearly lent Gilberto a black suit, the pant legs too long without his wife's attention to the hem. Troubled at the loss of his father, his sometime pal, with whom he once enjoyed a few daily beers in Neira bars, Gilberto was lost in his thoughts. Every year, he had bought his father a new felt hat for his birthday, to replace the old one that crumbled under an abusive sun beating down on him during his days selling cheese-and-honey turnovers in La Galería. *The old man is gone; he'll never hear of my suffering,* he thought, as he watched them lowering the coffin into the grave. *He had no opinions, but he bore faithful witness; never smiled, but enjoyed his life. He never prayed, yet was free of sins.* Gilberto would have liked to have inherited a little of his father's honesty and commitment, but no, everything had gone to pieces, and it was too late now. The only thing left was to emulate his wisdom and tact, to cope with what was left of his life.

María Sucel stayed near the group of main mourners, next to her mother-in-law, who was sorrowfully watching as they buried her husband. She stayed for the service, because she had always liked her father-in-law, though she was sure that all the Cervanteses had hidden the deception from her and she quietly hated them all. Analdo greeted her, and she responded out of politeness, but she didn't chat. It was the same with Sigifredo, Dora, and Romelia. When she found an opportunity, she offered Doña Sara her condolences and left before anyone else. Gilberto was aware of every move she made, but she acted as if she were alone. She disappeared as though she had come to the burial only to say goodbye to Don Acasio.

The '60s came to an end, and so did their once open and positive conversations, at least during those stormy days. A mute and isolated María Sucel barely acknowledged Gilberto's presence, for inevitably she could not deny he was the father of her eight children. Given her lack of attention, when he was home, he escaped into his most precious mental exile, the books by Kardec. When he wasn't home, he was perhaps taking care of Ophir, or God knows what. In the tense environment that they created and barely disguised in front of the children, Rosalía became the messenger between them. The old metal bed was his lone comfortable shelter, because she slept while holding her youngest every night, after putting them to bed early to avoid being alone with him.

One of those subsequent days, after she had sent the older children off to school, María Sucel approached the bed where he was sleeping and jerked the covers off. Exploding at last, her anguish burst forth in the form of demands. Life had changed so much that Gilberto barely paid the rent. Meals consisted of only one dish, without meat or dairy products, because they were expensive and because, due to non-payment, their credit with Don Antonio and at the Velardes' butcher shop had dried up. Seeing his wife's angry face, Gilberto reacted fearfully; she hadn't even given him time to feel cold.

"Where is the house that belongs to my children? Where is the money?" she shouted, inflamed. Gilberto hesitated in the face of such harsh words. He didn't know what to say, and once again let uncertainty take over. At his silence, she asked again, even more upset: "Where is my children's money? Please answer me!" She stood right in front of him, her eyes full of ire, her rapid panting hitting his face. He could not hide the truth; he would have to tell her what had happened, even if he knew it would destroy any remnant of stability left in that home.

Quietly, he said, "I lost it."

She had been ready for anything, except such a huge disappointment. In her thoughts, she shouted: *Imbecile!*

Walking to the wardrobe, she pulled out a skirt and a blouse, and ironed them on one of the beds under her husband's perplexed gaze. María Sucel took the pressed clothing, hung it over her right arm, and went to the bathroom. Under a cold shower, she roughly scrubbed every inch of her skin. Fully dressed, she entered the room again, pulled on a wool jacket and went out. Gilberto hugged the younger children, trying to comfort their aching souls after they had witnessed this altercation. He covered them with kisses and rocked them in silence. Without showering, he then got dressed and went out into the street, pushing the heavy metal cart with the few items he still had to sell. The challenge ahead was as huge and important as a bowl of soup for a starving man. Such was his life after constant setbacks.

It was late at night when, from a window, he spotted María Sucel two blocks away, walking towards the house. She carried a bundle in her right hand, and a large purse hung from her left shoulder. Without hesitation, he got into bed with one of his books, settled on the pillow and crossed his feet. Putting on his reading glasses, he opened the book to a random page, not actually intending to read it. When it occurred to him that she shouldn't arrive to find him reading, and thus think he was only interested in improving his mind, he changed strategies and pretended to be adding up some orders for the following day. He got up to look out the window again, and seeing that she was still at a certain distance, left the room and pulled a woolen blanket from under the plastic that protected the merchandise in the cart. He felt like an idiot for pretending to be doing something just so his wife would notice him, care for him. Then he thought, *God ... I don't think she'll have the slightest faith in me. Why wasn't I a better man before?* He carelessly threw the plastic back on the cart, and, aware that María Sucel would be arriving soon, ran to pick up little Juan de Dios, who was sleeping, like the rest of the children, in the middle of the crowded pile of mattresses. *I'll hold the boy, and she'll be touched; she'll think I take good care of them ... but if he wakes up and cries, she'll think that it's my fault.* Time was running out, and so were his ideas. Lost in his anguished thoughts, he just ran to the bed and threw on his pajamas, got under the covers, and pretended to sleep.

When he finally heard María Sucel's steps outside, it was almost midnight. Gilberto heard her open the first lock on the gate, and then the second one; he heard his wife come inside and then lock up again. He heard her secure both locks, and then the iron bar, which she had to place because she was the last one to come inside, and they had to ensure the protection of the other families that slept in the rooming house in that big city. That city, where everyone knew that burglars came into homes to take everything they could find. Gilberto recognized each of her movements from their sound, as if he were seeing them. In his blanket shell, he had left a space to peek out at her once she entered the room. Fortunately, his bed was in a corner from which he could easily watch her.

María Sucel rushed straight into the kitchen they shared with other tenants in this house they had moved to a week earlier, escaping the financial pressures they were facing. She held a large bundle in one hand: a red and white checkered tablecloth she had knotted closed around the contents. Untying it, she took out delicious, carefully prepared food. There was a shrimp loaf, chicken, excellent cuts of beef. Placing them in a basket as though this was a picnic, she took the food into the room where the children slept. Awakening them one by one with gentle kisses on their cheeks and rubbing their little backs softly, speaking to them tenderly, she showed them the food, to which they reacted immediately. Gilberto peeked through the opening he had left between his covers, which disconnected him from a fascinating event to which he had not been invited. He watched as she bid them be quiet, to avoid waking him. He was calm, because the children had gone to bed hungry and he felt a wistful happiness for them from his blanket shelter. Following their satisfied movements, he watched them, even with their mouths full, competing about who could eat the most. "They'll have food even in their hair," he thought, as nobody was using the forks she had left next to the basket. There were plenty of fingers to pull apart the pieces of chicken, which they eagerly chose according to size. It had been several months since they had eaten meat. Now they ate until they were stuffed, then took turns kissing and thanking their mother, who truly enjoyed the attention. Apparently, she had stolen the delicious food from the kitchen where she worked as a servant. When they were done, she changed into her robe and settled into bed next to little Juan de Dios, hugging him tightly before falling deeply asleep for the next five hours, when she'd get up again to begin another day like this one. Their bellies full, they all went back to sleep.

They slept soundly, but he did not. Since the day he'd paid the past-due rent to the woman who had revealed the truth about Ophir, he'd suffered chronic insomnia. Silently, he waited for sleep to come to him. He thought about his loneliness, and how to recover his wife, or at least awaken in her some consideration that would break through her indifference. It was the same every single night. She neither knew nor cared that Gilberto was wallowing in memories and hoped that she would acknowledge him with a gesture or a glance. He could barely get any information from the children, or from Rosalía, who would meekly tell him about her adoptive mother's activities. He didn't dare approach María Sucel.

Months passed, and the Cervantes Baroja family became nomads on the northwest side of the capital. They changed boarding houses frequently because of the costs and deplorable living conditions. The family's fragile existence was gripped in chaos, and danger stalked their daily lives. Circumstances threatened their chance of survival. The children studied amid a profound crisis they didn't understand and that increasingly confused them. The cold, cement-floored rooms they occupied were dirty and neglected. At night, fleas feasted on their bodies; they would turn on the light to hunt them down and squeeze them between their thumbnails. The old, sagging mattresses smelled of urine. They became experts at finding the lice that overran their scalps—for entertainment, like apes. Despite the upheaval, they never stopped going to school, for it was much more fun and less monotonous than staying home. They continued to smile, despite being surrounded by neglect. They had become accustomed now to missing meals or surviving on sweetened water. Malnutrition made them thinner, and tartar covered their teeth. Gilberto, no longer at the helm, was unable to overcome the family's dire straits. He struggled to get his business going, amid a deeply rooted sadness that stubbornly resisted resignation. María Sucel always arrived home late at night, occasionally carrying bundles of leftover food that she had collected and clothes she received for the children. Bent double by fatigue and the lack of opportunities offered by the city, she was unable to obtain any better-paying work.

Sadness engulfed them; everything was getting worse and worse. Rosalía, the eleventh member of the Cervantes Baroja family by adoption, was pregnant after an encounter with another tenant. This was in a house in the Florencia neighborhood, where they had ended up, after much roaming, to escape the months of back rent they owed in other houses. The guy that got her pregnant was a bad sort named Ezequiel, and in the chaotic environment in which they were floundering, she was an easy mark. She submitted to him, overwhelmed by his advances and tired of living the way they had been in those days. The guy disappeared after the baby was born, and Gilberto offered to give the child his name, thinking to somehow repay Rosalía's faithful service over the years. But Rosalía left, taking her little boy with her. It was said the guy showed up again, guitar in hand, drunkenly serenading her with his friends at all hours, and the songs of that urban minstrel had bewitched her ears. Ezequiel took her to live on the south side of Bogotá, to a neighborhood as miserable as the ones she had known in the past. In the end, he went to prison for killing two others in a fight. Rosalía's departure deepened the crisis, leaving Piedad, Maru, and Sara, who were only eleven, ten, and eight, completely in charge of the home during the day. They also had to manage the little money that Gilberto gave them before he went out to sell whatever merchandise other vendors occasionally provided him. The girls had to squeeze every penny for supplies to make broth or to buy sugar cane to sweeten the water with which they eased their hunger for long hours.

The day before Mother's Day in 1972, the three youngest brothers, Cesarino, Acasio Elías, and Juan de Dios, were walking down a dusty street full of potholes filled with stagnant rainwater. They were struggling to drag home a burlap bag filled with scrap iron, tin cans, copper wire, and cardboard they had found in garbage cans. A neighbor's mother, who had survived for decades as a "disposable"—the term applied in Bogotá to street kids and beggars who sift through trash—had told them these things could be sold. Around two in the afternoon, Gilberto was walking slowly down the same street, pushing his cart, and hurried to catch up with them when he saw them dragging the bag of junk. The boys greeted him cheerfully, full of enthusiasm, but were dumbstruck when he furiously took the heavy bag from them and hurled it away. Frightened, their faces fell as they stared at him, trying to understand his behavior. Their father pulled off his belt and wrapped it around his right hand, threatening them.

"I will punish you for collecting garbage! That's not what I've taught you!"

He whipped Cesarino, who curled himself up in terror like a scaly pangolin. Gilberto, imprisoned in his sadness, had exploded at seeing that what he had built with his life resembled nothing he had ever imagined. The old man, beaten down now, was becoming aggressive. It was as though bitterness had sunk its teeth deep into him, driving him toward something like insanity. In those days, not even Ophir made an appearance. Faced with their father's fury, the other two little brothers wanted to run away, but they were paralyzed by fear. Gilberto finally came to his senses and stopped, no longer recognizing himself in his own behavior. He began shivering in shame and was deeply repentant.

"Forgive me, son. Come here, come. The last thing I want is to punish you. Go on home, I'll be right there. We'll talk about what you should and shouldn't do. Did your mother give you permission to go out alone and collect junk?" he asked them.

"No, sir," answered Cesarino, halfway between a sob and a grimace. "She doesn't know."

"We want money for a gift for Mother's Day," whimpered Acasio Elías.

"I want to buy her a rose. She likes them ..." added Juan de Dios, innocently. He was also crying.

"All right, all right. I hate to see you becoming disposables," he grumbled. "You won't understand what I'm talking about. Come with me to put the cart away, and leave that junk there, you won't be needing it. Let's have chicken for lunch at a nearby restaurant. What do you think?" The boys jumped for joy. Eating chicken would be wonderful, especially because their father was paying and they could have their fill. Juan de Dios hugged his leg, and Gilberto rubbed Cesarino's arm where he had hit him, and apologized with deep affection.

"Later we'll go to buy flowers, a card, and some chocolates. What do you say?"

Acasio Elías and Cesarino climbed on the cart. They chatted as they walked, and Gilberto enjoyed their company as he tried to persuade them not to repeat this outing that had so embarrassed him. He knew neighborhood boys who did such things, and who smoked marijuana and inhaled glue or gasoline to forget their miserable lives.

Nothing changed after that day, nor did María Sucel

hear about it. The family's days continued as before. Gilberto took refuge in the room where he kept his merchandise, while she spent long days mopping and cleaning floors in various businesses. She worked under the supervision of Don Rafael, a boastful boss who promised the humble cleaning women heaven and earth while paying them meager wages below the government-approved minimum. The work day began at six in the morning and ended when it ended, no guarantees. They had only Sundays off to share with their children. Gilberto continued his work as a spiritist, praying for himself and for others.

When Picasso Died

...1973

The frustration of María Sucel's constant indifference clung to him like a tick. To avoid it, he moved to a rented room, a kind of storage space for merchandise that was located only a few blocks' walk away, so he could stop by to see his children. At this point, she no longer cared.

On one of those rough days in the 1970s, Gilberto was lying in bed at five in the morning, cold and full of bitterness. It was dark outside. The radio had become his best friend, a privilege he enjoyed together with unfiltered cigarettes and a box of matches. Every morning, an early news broadcast provided a compass for the new day.

«*Attention, attention. Broadcasting for our nationwide audience, attention ...*»

He had another half-hour to laze in bed before it was time to get up. The announcer read the news with the same intonation used by snake-oil salesmen in Las Nieves Plaza, who touted potions to cure the effects of an evil eye or rid pale children of their tapeworms.

«*Attention, attention ... Bucaramanga, attention ... Five soldiers were killed in an ambush yesterday at dawn, by an armed group presumed to be the ELN, in the Cimitarra region, Santander, the Fifth Brigade command headquartered in Bucaramanga has stated.»*

Gilberto uncovered his face, searched for a cigarette, and lit it.

«Attention, attention ... Paris, attention ... The world-renowned Spanish artist Pablo Ruiz Picasso has died of a pulmonary edema today, April 8th, 1973, at the age of 91, in his home on the French Riviera. His wife, Jacqueline, age 46, was with him at the time of his death, and his oldest son, Paolo, his private secretary, and several persons close to the family.»

"Picasso is dead. He must be at peace. Much more than me," he said, exhaling cigarette smoke.

«Attention, attention ... Bogotá, attention ... A man set himself and his five children on fire in Bogotá. Attention. The horrifying murder-suicide took place on Thursday night, when, in despair that his wife had abandoned them, the father poured gasoline on himself and his five little ones. The tragedy has shaken the Egipto neighborhood.»

Hearing this news item, he thought about himself, and María Sucel, and his torment. He could almost understand that immolated father's motivation. He thought about it, and then his reaction over such a horrible event concerned him.

Scratching his head and his unshaven chin, now sprinkled with gray, he inhaled cigarette smoke deeply, then threw the butt on the floor to burn itself out. Throwing aside the covers, he walked to the small section of the room set aside for washing. He splashed his face with cold water, ran his wet hands through his hair and combed it; he didn't bother to shave, nobody cared. Dressed in his old, sun-faded suit, he went out to a nearby coffee shop for his morning coffee, from there to begin pushing his cart at a snail's pace, in the hopes that some customer would approach to buy something. At noon, the sky turned gray and a slight rain-soaked breeze sent him indoors. Deciding that he was finished working for the day, an hour later he was back in his room, a few new sales on his card. Minutes later, having skipped lunch, he went to a bar, asked for a coffee and a pool table, and for long hours practiced pool shots, his cigarette dangling from his lips. One drink followed another, and the weight of day began to crush him until he was sitting at a table surrounded by empty glasses and ashes. The girl who waited on him knew him, and she knew that at ten she would have to wake him up and ask him to pay his bill.

He left the bar, shivering from the cold, and walked along the street to a chicken rotisserie, where he ordered some chicken pieces. He stumbled several more blocks to the boarding house where his children were sleeping. Opening the gate with his key, he walked down the dark corridor to the end and entered a room. His children stirred when he made noise, bumbling around drunkenly, and turned on the light. One by one, they began to wake up. He offered them chicken, imitating those nights when his wife would wake them up to feed them. While they ate, he kissed their heads, leaving the stink of his drunkenness on everything he touched. A few minutes after their dinner, he urged them to go back to bed. They did so promptly, for the night's chill beckoned them under the covers, and they immediately fell into deep sleep.

It was eleven now, and María Sucel still wasn't home. She was cleaning for a finance company in a new skyscraper at that time. In his drunken state, Gilberto was erratic. Any other day, he'd already be sleeping in his room; tonight, feeling sentimental and depressed, he wanted to be near his children. Sitting there in the dark, trapped again in his loneliness, despair washed over him. He needed to speak with María Sucel, to tell her how much he needed her, but the minutes passed, and she didn't come home. His face turned ugly, which didn't bode well. Looking at the walls, his eyes kept returning to a photograph taken in mid-1958, to María Sucel's lovely figure standing next to him. He was starting to go crazy, thinking listlessly that this was all about María Sucel, trying vainly to move ahead with their lives by any means, thwarted by fate.

Agonized, wandering like a ghost in the middle of the night, Gilberto went to the kitchen and found the biggest, sharpest knife. Hiding it under his ruana, he went into the bathroom. As he looked at his reflection in the medicine cabinet mirror, he saw his own decay, just as monstrous as he had remembered. The fateful morning news item about the self-immolated jealous father galloped through his hazy mind. But he refused to think further about it, and this perverse impulse was defeated. He broke into inconsolable tears, curled up on the toilet in a fetal position. He waited, immobile, letting his self-recriminations shred what was left of his self-esteem. After a while, he walked into the children's room and took down the wedding photo, an image with the Sacred Heart of Jesus, another of Jesus of Nazareth, and one of St. Expeditus. He carried them to the bathroom and huddled there, with his head between his knees.

At midnight, a woman's heels tapped rapid steps outside, followed by the noise of the gate. The cold made María Sucel's nose run. A purse hung from her arm and her left hand held a bundle, as usual, with some things for her little ones. She smelled food as she entered the room. Tiptoeing to the small bed where she slept with Juan de Dios, she covered his little face with the sheet before turning on a light, one that emitted a dim glow. She looked at each child and saw the leftover chicken. Guessing that Gilberto had brought food, she felt content to know they were fed. Taking off her costume pearl earrings and her wedding ring, she put them in a box in her wardrobe. Then she undressed, put on her robe, and looked towards the image of the Sacred Heart to give thanks for one more day—but all she saw was the wall. Searching for an explanation, she imagined that one of the children had taken it down to copy it in a drawing, for they sometimes did that with other pictures. She noted that the picture of Jesus of Nazareth was also missing, and St. Expeditus, and her wedding photo. Something strange was going on, she thought. She crossed herself, praying to God for protection from evil and danger, and decided that instead of waking any of her children up, she would think about it a bit more. She pulled on a wool sweater as she headed for the bathroom before bed. In the small patio that led to the bathroom, she came face-to-face with her trembling husband, his gray eyes unfocused and reflecting the crazed crisis into which he had fallen.

She screamed in fear, and he quickly grabbed her arm and dragged her to the bathroom, the knife in his hand glinting with each movement. María Sucel was speechless, petrified by this assault, and, entrusting herself to God, submitted to his shouting. He shoved her against the toilet; she resisted quietly to avoid causing panic, and he turned on the light. As she watched in terror, he took their wedding photo and smashed it violently against the wall, the loud noise waking everyone in the boarding house. Doors began to open, scared faces peeking out as lights went on in the rooms. Gilberto kicked at the pictures of the Sacred Heart and the Nazarene, destroying them while shouting insults. The drama escalated; the children wailed outside the bathroom door. Not a single word passed María Sucel's lips as she tried simply to protect herself. Although Gilberto pushed and shoved her, he did not hit her. He behaved like a coward, the kind that only makes noise because all they need is attention.

His festering inner anguish had burst like an infection when he understood that he had lost María Sucel and was unable to do anything except watch it happen. The neighbors finally managed to quiet him down and took him to another tenant's room; the women took care of María Sucel's bruises. The police arrived and took Gilberto away; María Sucel refused to hear a word from him, and he gave up.

Because of the tremendous love they had for their children, calmness returned to their lives. He gave up drinking; he seemed to settle down after that night, as if he had hit bottom, and had turned to God. He remained a quite respected spiritist, something that had always comforted him. Time passed, and the room where he lived a few blocks from our home became a true shrine where, every afternoon, people visited him from all over the city, referred by others. Many of them, terminally ill, traveled from faraway places on the plains, so he would pray over them and rid them of their pain.

In the mid-'70s, the family moved several times. By then, María Sucel had become capable of obtaining, quite efficiently, whatever they needed. Toñito and Tomás were no longer children; they had grown tall. Learning of their tremendous need, the headmaster of El Parroquial befriended María Sucel, and thanks to his kindness, lucky Tomás, the second oldest, ended up living at the boarding school. Occasionally, Gilberto would stop by the school to give him a few coins to spend and to say hello. Despite the situation, he never abandoned any of the children.

On a certain Saturday night, María Sucel was primping in front of the mirror, with all the care demanded by the special invitation she had received. She was overcome with emotion about it. There was something surreal about this evening, for it had been many years since she had thought about actually having fun, having been fully dedicated to working hard to pull her children out of the hole they had fallen into.

For this occasion, she had ordered an elegant black dress made with fabric she had bought on sale, nothing expensive. A woman she had met at work came to fix her makeup. María Sucel looked radiant. She wore lipstick, and her eyes looked pretty and bright under her long eyelashes. Her daughters enthusiastically helped her roll up her sheer stockings, zipped up her dress, and polished her high-heeled leather shoes, which made her look elegant and graceful.

"He's here! He's here!" someone shouted excitedly. María Sucel took one more look in the mirror, kissed each of the children, and left. That day, she didn't look like a mother of eight but rather a young and attractive woman from the neighborhood. There was Tomás, waiting to take her to a fundraiser at the school hall, where a band hired by the school would entertain the guests. Courteously, respectfully, Tomás opened the rear door of the taxi, with a gentlemanly bow that made her feel good. She got in happily, feeling confident, and waved and threw kisses to those watching her leave.

Arriving at El Parroquial, they encountered a crowd waiting to enter the ballroom. In the distance they could hear the band tuning their instruments. Shyly, happily, María Sucel enjoyed the moment as if she were a young girl. At the threshold, she stopped to look around at everything before entering. The partygoers' joy spoke magically to her, but inexperience made her timid, and she hung on to Tomás's arm. Feeling very proud of her, he escorted her through the room until they reached a special table near the band, where other boarding students were sitting next to the headmaster, Mr. Cuacazo, and his wife, Lulu.

The boys and the headmaster got to their feet when they arrived at the table. Blushing at their respectful attitude, María Sucel extended her right hand to greet each one in turn. Lulu rescued her, saying, "Sit here next to me, so we can chat."

"Thank you, Lulu, you're most kind." Proudly explaining that Tomás was quickly becoming a man and escorting her for the first time, she thanked Mr. Cuacazo for this invitation.

"It's our pleasure, Doña María. But don't concern yourself about it. It's time to enjoy yourself, please. By the way, what would you like to drink?"

"Just a soft drink, thank you."

"A soft drink?" he exclaimed in surprise.

"Yes, sir. I don't drink anything stronger that could make me act foolishly. Drinking is for men."

"I agree," added Mrs. Lulu. "They seem to think they can only have a good time if they drink. I prefer music with a soft drink."

"Then, if you don't want to drink liquor, please, have

a President," Cuacazo offered courteously.

"I'm sorry, Mr. Cuacazo. I don't smoke, either. It makes me cough."

"Well, you should at least dance. The band is excellent! They've practiced a lot and always enliven these events," the headmaster said.

"If I told you that I don't know how to dance, you'll laugh, but it's the truth," she confessed.

"Don't worry, Mother, I'll teach you," announced Tomás. "If you can't dance when you live on the coast, you're truly screwed—sorry, I meant to say, *lost*. With these coastal folks, I've learned to move only my feet, or I should say my legs, because according to these *guajiros*, jumping is the way inland *cachacos* dance. And though we are *cachacos*, I like the idea of dancing like a coastal man."

"Do you like the kind of music called *vallenato*?" asked Cuacazo, with regional pride.

"I don't know what that is, could you explain it to me?" requested María Sucel.

"It's the music that Juancho Polo Valencia sings. Haven't you heard the one that goes *'Sí, sí, sí vivo paseando en Santa Marta. Sí, sí, sí, la capital del Magdalena …'*"

"I'm so sorry, I've never heard it, but I'm sure that Tomás will teach me a bit," she replied cheerfully.

"I'll ask the band to play a slow *vallenato*, so you can try it, and get warmed up."

"You're all so kind. But, please, go ahead and dance. Maybe as I watch you from here, I can learn a bit."

"Try it, Mother. Let's dance," suggested Tomás, taking her hand. "It doesn't matter whether we do it well." But, embarrassed, she refused once again.

As the party got under way, María Sucel finally agreed

to go out on the crowded dance floor, seeing that everyone was dancing. She soon became more confident, enjoying her son's attentive instruction, and in no time, she was dancing fairly well. Two hours later, she was cheerfully remembering parties in Armenia when she was a youngster. Her son's friends constantly asked her to dance, amid laughter, fun, and the ubiquitous conga lines; with a couple of rum-and-Cokes in her system, she was feeling very good. It was a night like no other; she hadn't had that much fun since they celebrated her son Cesarino's baptism in Armenia with a party that lasted until dawn.

At around three in the morning, her son suggested they go for a walk in the school gardens, as many other guests had. The night was chilly, but bearable.

"I've brought a light rum drink for us to share while we're outside, to refresh ourselves," he said.

"That's a good idea, but I didn't know that you were already drinking liquor. You're still very young!" she commented sharply. Tomás smiled but ignored her. He had already made up his mind to be an adult and make his own decisions. They walked among other people and chatted.

"I'm proud to have gotten you out of the house for some fun, like the times we would have when you and Father still spoke to each other."

"I miss those days, too, though they seem impossible now. That's life."

"Do you feel something missing at a time like this?"

The young mother was silent a while. "Don't ask me that, son. I don't want to ruin this lovely evening. It's best to leave well enough alone," she said.

"Mother, life will change. We'll grow up, and together we'll help you to push forward. Maybe that way, you and

Father will be able to have a better future …"

"He should be here, dancing with me, having a drink and a good time. But he preferred to wallow in his miserable failure and escape with Kardec into the plains, as he has done ever since he dragged us to Bogotá. He isolates himself every time, always further away, resolving nothing, just struggling to bring in food. It's never enough; he doesn't fight to reshape his destiny," declared María Sucel. She continued looking up at the moon over Bogotá, finally lowering her gaze.

"Will you ever forgive him, Mother?" Tomás asked her.

"Forgiveness doesn't bring happiness; it's only something decent people do. But forgiving doesn't guarantee that you'll forget. It would be like trying to find warmth in the morning rain of this asphalt city, instead of feeling sun where the coffee grows."

"You're not old yet; what will happen with what's left of your youth?" wondered her son.

"It will follow the usual pace of life, God willing. But let's talk about something less lofty. This is a magical night, and on magical nights there shouldn't be scary life truths."

"If it was in our power to see you two reconciled, we would fight for it," insisted Tomás, unwilling to drop the subject.

"We're separated, you know that. Totally separated. We just keep frequenting the same place where our children live, because we're completely separated from each other but not from our children, who we love deeply."

"Are you saying that you maintain this absurd situation because of us?"

"The love for one's children is greater than other kinds

of love."

"And does Father think the same as you do? Does he also live like this because of his love for us?"

"I don't know. Ask him yourself; you see him more than I do."

"Is life all about resentment?"

"You sound like an adult, asking such grown-up questions. Let's go back inside and dance some more." She looked at him with tenderness, not forgetting that she was his mother on this evening that felt like a date.

"Someday we'll only be history, and none of this will mean a thing," she said. "The past has more power than the present, but today it seems possible to leave it behind. Let's look towards tomorrow. What I feel for your father is very strange. I wouldn't call it resentment, but rather sadness. That's it, sadness. I think it's the word that best replaces frustration. You should all love him very much, for you are his only reason for living."

"Others love him very much. For example, the patients who visit him for spiritism. They even call him Brother Gilberto."

"That's funny," she said, and smiled somewhat sarcastically. Tomás took a deep breath, and hugged her. They went inside and danced, celebrating their affection.

Dawn dispelled the enchantment of the night, magically escorting their two shadows on the street that Sunday morning. Everyone was still sleeping when they arrived home, exhausted. Before going to bed, María Sucel warmed up some coffee and took a cup to her son. But she was too late; he had already fallen into a deep, bottomless sleep.

Farewell to the Older Ones

...1977

At 6 a.m. María Sucel was on the long-distance bus to Armenia, where she arrived at 2 p.m., alone, at the address written on a piece of notepaper. She walked down well-remembered streets, recognizing some businesses. Some people greeted her; she recognized others but didn't greet them for fear that they might have forgotten her. She was excited to arrive.

According to the address, the Barojas lived in Corbones, but she had never imagined that the directions would lead her to a cliff, difficult to reach over a soft dirt road. A boy helped her locate the slum where she was headed, the only option available in that area. Sadly, she realized that her folks had also fallen into poverty over the past few years. Climbing the steep rise as best she could, she saw a shack made of adobe with dark rooms. In the doorway, she saw Gabriel, a man now, carelessly dressed, his face looking strange and his manner dismissive.

Approaching him, she greeted him enthusiastically. "Hello, Gabriel! My, how you've changed! I'm so glad to see you!" She embraced him tightly, but he remained tense, disconcertingly timid.

"Hello, Aunt. How are you?" he replied tersely.

"Fine, fine. How is my father?"

"Well," he said, "you'll see. Go on, he's inside with Mother Isabelina."

Suddenly remorseful, she felt an ominous chill in the air. Entering, she saw an aged Isabelina with a woven mantle covering her head. She sat next to an icy Elías, keeping vigil by the light of a candle. When death had caught up with Elías, he had been living in absolute poverty, without the means to engage a funeral home.

María Sucel walked slowly and spoke to her quietly. "Mama."

Isabelina turned, and seeing her, walked up, and they kissed each other's cheek.

She sadly said, "He waited for you, child. He said he wanted to say goodbye, but he could hang on no longer. He left his love and blessings for his Marujita."

Unable to hide her sorrow, his daughter struggled to hold back an explosion of emotion. Turning to look at that pale figure, time stood still. She remembered when she would chase Elías endlessly, and, vigorous then, he would pick her up so she could kiss him. She thought of him, sad and frustrated by his fear of aging alone, and she felt guilty. Inevitably, her thoughts returned to how she had rejoiced when her father overcame his apprehensions about Gilberto and thanked God that she had not told her father about his resounding failure. Her eyes were glued to the figure of the elderly man, who had taken to his death knowledge he had never spoken of. Overcome with profound grief, she took his hands and kissed them repeatedly; she kissed his forehead, and said The Lord's Prayer. Isabelina continued to grieve silently, alone.

After weeping for many long minutes, María Sucel took care of preparations for the funeral. With some ropes and their neighbors' help, the coffin was taken down the hill, and a procession of about fifteen people accompanied it to the cemetery. Bertha showed up. María Sucel tossed a flower on her father's coffin, as he had asked her to do when she had seen him last, on the day they had been uprooted to the capital. But it wasn't the only one; the few mourners also threw in flowers. In the evening, they began a novena, and for the next few days the family gathered on that awful cliff. Then they dispersed.

Bertha persuaded Isabelina to stay with them in Manizales for a while. Gabriel remained at the mercy of the marijuana addiction that now invaded his days and his nights, and after that, nobody heard from Gabriel again. That very same year, Eliseo was also taken from them, leaving Bertha a widow with a stable family. It was as if Eliseo had gone to keep Elías company. María Sucel sent a votive offering by mail and phoned from a booth where long-distance service was available to offer her condolences and comfort them with her voice and words of encouragement. She promised to pray for his soul at mass. A few months later in that funereal year, death came in Bogotá, hitting Gilberto, his siblings, and their children deeply. They buried Doña Sara, who had thrashed him when he was twenty. She had succumbed to emphysema, brought on by her habit of smoking in peaceful times or stressful ones.

Everyone who believes in Him shall not perish but have eternal life, the La Granja church choir sang on a Thursday, when she calculated that the dates of her deceased coincided. María Sucel had paid Father Jaime a pretty penny to pray at that day's mass for the souls of those who had gone, especially for Elías, for whose death without her presence brought everlasting remorse.

Days later, María Sucel managed to settle into a more permanent post, though it involved cleaning toilets in the supply office of an important financial company. She worked out of a basement where she clocked in every morning at five. After cleaning all the offices, she prepared coffee and herbals for an army of workers. This was history repeating itself, for in the late 1930s Isabelina had taken care of a camp full of road workers, feeding them and seeing to their comfort. Cleaning and serving had become her chief means of survival, a way to overcome adversity. Her delicate demeanor, added to her pleasant appearance, made her likable to anyone who saw her, even though she was simply a cleaning woman. Everyone who knew her called her Doña María, or sometimes Mistress María. Antonio, who was eighteen already and worked on scaffolding as a skyscraper window-washer, had gotten a job on the night shift in a city radio station that few people listened to. They tuned in to that station only to hear the announcer mention Antonio as the technician, the one turning the knobs. In other words, he was the person in charge of playing the vinyl records all night long, according to a list handed to him at the beginning of his shift.

One of those gray days common in Bogotá dawned, bringing hope for a new beginning for Gilberto. His black leather shoes were beat up from the previous day, and he attempted to give them a shinier appearance with a wet rag. They shone where there weren't any cracks in the seams, but you could still see the effects of the dust and the resistant dry mud stains from a few days earlier. He had washed his shirt in the bathroom sink, since the room didn't have a laundry area, and it had dried on a clothes hanger in the bathroom. It still felt damp and stiff from the cold. Resigned, he pushed his arms into the sleeves despite the cold contact against his skin. After this daily ritual, he left the room at about seven, in search of coffee and time to think before returning to pick up the cart.

Entering a neighborhood called La Clarita, he stopped in front of one of those urban houses that still had small gardens, this one scattered with rosebushes but overrun with weeds and grass. He looked in all directions and, seeing that no one was about, carefully broke off a stem with a tight, red rosebud. Then, he took up a fistful of wet earth and covered the broken part of the stem. Gilberto hid his stolen rose among his wares, careful not to damage the flower's innate beauty. He walked on, his memory repeating episodes of his life. He made a couple of sales, earning enough cash to save the day. Then, flushed with happiness, he arrived home. Greeting those who were home already, he went to the kitchen to find an empty bottle, like the ones used for cooking oil, and washed it with soap and water. Filling it halfway with water, he carefully took the rose and placed it there, so it rested prettily. Lastly, he took it to María Sucel's room and wiped the surface before setting it on the dresser. The rose held its shape for several days before it shriveled. Gilberto often looked at that bottle, pondering the lack of reaction to it that exhibited her indifference, and felt only emptiness.

The following week, another rose appeared in the same place, and likewise succumbed to the arrogance of time. Every week, the roses arrived silently, then bent their necks, growing darker, shedding their petals on the wooden surface. Occasionally, one of the daughters would offer an affectionate compliment, and these he accepted as spontaneous reactions to the blooms' beauty, not as evidence of their love towards the one regularly bringing the roses. Only once, he noticed Piedad smelling their fragrance.

The roses were increasingly noted, to the point that even María Sucel, who had been pretending not to care, had wondered about their provenance. One of the girls claimed their father had been stealing from gardens, while another said that his sweetheart gave them to him. Laughing, María Sucel downplayed any speculation, exhibiting some level of inner peace about it.

Gilberto had learned not to pay attention to any of their comments. He had become someone who was always floating in the family's space but had no opinions, who was available in the evenings to those seeking prayers or an exorcism. The roses were a constant, persistent presence, now held in a transparent glass bud vase he had bought in Plaza España when acquiring merchandise.

The prevailing sentiment towards the intransigent roses was expressed by silence. Peace and indifference went hand in hand in this home, as they had within a few short months after this began. What was different now was the children's continued development. Their success in school gave everyone incentive. Mother had good friends at work, and the family breathed easier, though they continued to live in northwestern neighborhoods where she knew the streets and the families.

Gilberto had temporarily given up spiritist consultations, though every day people continued to come, asking him for help with their troubles. All these years later, he had set out to make amends for the loss of the house in

El Paraíso, and in rough territory. For the past two months he had traveled every day to the very south of the capital, hours away on the city bus. There, in the middle of a muddy lot and with Cesarino's help, he worked on digging the foundation for a small shack. At thirteen, Cesarino had become an unquestioning companion, following him on the streets on a small bicycle, or helping to push the cart. After a few months, Gilberto thought he was ready for the Cervantes family to move into their own house in Bogotá. He planned to tell his wife that the humble house would belong to them all, and that he would ask them to move in the following month.

One Sunday afternoon, when everyone was home, Cesarino spoke to his mother.

"Father wants to give us a surprise, Mother, but it's important that you listen to him. He asks that you please give him just a few minutes to tell you about the house that is almost ready."

María Sucel thought about it. She was ashamed that one of her children was asking permission for his father to speak to her. She felt the weight of obligation as everyone looked on, their eyes silently begging for her consent. It was Sara who spoke first.

"Please, Mother. A few minutes won't hurt. It wouldn't be fair to ignore such a noble gesture."

"It's not right to stay silent when he's gone to such effort," Cesarino added.

"Tell him I'll be right there," she replied when she saw how her children's eyes shone with hope.

Cesarino smiled and shared a sly look with the others. Their mother stepped into the bathroom while Cesarino walked to the back room, where Gilberto was listening to the radio. He stood when his son entered, without taking the cigarette from his lips.

"She's coming, Dad."

Cesarino walked out as María Sucel came in, looking serious but serene. Gilberto offered her a seat on the bed. She sat, looking at him surreptitiously, hoping she wouldn't have to look him in the eyes.

"What do you want?" she asked tersely.

"A few years ago, when I lost our savings, I realized that the toughest days were still ahead. I set out to recover a shred of dignity for my children, and penny by penny, I was able to obtain a small parcel of land on the south side of the city. I've scraped some money together, which allowed me to build something. It's to the south, far from here, but in the city itself. I've worked at leveling the land with Cesarino's help, and sometimes with Acasio Elías and Juan de Dios. We've set the foundation to build a small house that will be ours from now on. It's humble, like all the ones surrounding us, and cold, like that room I took you to the first day we arrived from Armenia. It's strange because, though it's in Bogotá, the neighborhood is poorer than the places we've lived. There aren't any neighbors, so it's lonely. But I and the three boys have put all our sweat into each wall of it. Before I die, I want to make amends, at least a little, for the damage I've done to the future of all of you." He took a deep breath, pulled up a chair, and sat calmly facing them.

Moved, María Sucel held her right cheek, her thoughts drifting into the past.

"It's not the palace you deserve. That only existed in El Paraíso," he stated sadly. "In this cold shack, which will also be ours, perhaps there might be flowers like the ones that linger in your memory. I will continue to struggle until my last breath."

She remained calm and kept her eyes down. When Gilberto finally finished speaking, she looked at him. For a fleeting instant, she noticed that his once lively gray eyes had become sad and melancholy. Remembering that she hadn't looked into those eyes for over a decade, despite sharing the same roof, she tried to remain unaffected.

"I will speak to the children, for everything you want to share belongs to them. They're grown now and will much appreciate your effort," she replied, blushing. She stood and left the room. Her husband lit a cigarette and went back to listening to the usual station, where through his music Olimpo Cárdenas transported him back to the coffee shops in La Galería in Armenia.

And they tried it. They left in a slat-sided truck full of household belongings, during what was the school break for most of the youngsters.

The new house was cold and lonely, the nights freezing, the neighborhood inhospitable and scary. Moving to that place might have been the most daring family endeavor yet, a major effort to support Gilberto's attempt to soften the anguish of their family breakdown. They lived there a few days, dealing with all kinds of problems. They had to get up at 4 a.m. in order to arrive on time to work and school.

But after a few months, they had given up on the idea of settling down in the south, the greatest challenge being the family's fear over exposing the girls to danger. Drugs and alcohol ran rampant in the the neighborhood, so this initiative by Gilberto touched each of their lives. Since the two eldest already had good jobs, Gilberto was easily persuaded to sell the house. They would move again, paying rent somewhere less dangerous and warmer. The family, headed by María Sucel, and including the older sons and Gilberto as well, decided to find a house together in the northwest, with more rooms, where they would all fit. Gilberto would finally come back home, no matter that things related to love had been stored away as yesterday's memories.

"You'll have a room of your own to sleep, Father. We're happy! Mother agrees, she never told you to leave, you did that on your own. The family will be together—the two of you, the eight of us. We'll have room for your wares, too, for your bicycle and your sales cart. There will be room to put José Gregorio Hernández, as well, and the altar for praying," they said, planning it all out with enthusiasm.

"I'd like to think about it a little," he replied.

He went out to the street and got on an almost empty city bus towards the northwest. The trip would take a while, enough time to think. He was optimistic. The rapprochement he and María Sucel had been having seemed miraculous, like the affection his children had been showing him. Getting off the bus in the Boyacá neighborhood, he walked along streets he knew well from pushing his cart full of wares. He visited several houses for rent, even meeting a few of the owners. He selected three of them to consider, bursting with happiness. It was dark when he returned to the south, to wait for his wife to get home from work. When she arrived, he asked her politely for a few minutes of time before she went to bed, to talk. She agreed.

"I found three large houses, in Boyacá and in Palo Blanco. The owners will meet us, so we can see them together. When do you think we could go?"

"Tomorrow afternoon I'll ask for time off, and we can meet around one, all right?" She went into the room where she and the girls slept uncomfortably packed together. He went to the other room, where all the boys slept in placid confusion. These difficult days, he thought, might be a harbinger of better days ahead, of greater closeness. Still chasing the magical illusion that, in the end, María Sucel would take him back, for Gilberto, perseverance would bring a sweet reward. He hadn't met with her for a very long time. Their presence only coincided on occasion— to celebrate the end of the school year, or at some birthday, or at Christmas. This date was important, for there would have to be some kind of conversation, however brief. At fifty-seven, Gilberto had become excessively cautious, even with his children, whose futures he was just beginning to imagine. Adults now, his sons were his friends; there was no more shame to cover up, and they still spoke with a certain frivolity.

He was the first to arrive at their appointment, feeling the way he had as a youngster when he had managed to get a date with one of the coffee picker girls. The difference was that, this time, there was no gel in his hair and his skin was no longer youthful. What Gilberto felt at that moment was like the moment when Elías had finally let him through the door to court María Sucel. When she finally arrived, Gilberto watched her as she got off the bus and thought wistfully of the beautiful woman that he had had forever; the one he had been careless of, and lost; the one who had given him eight children.

"Hello, Gilberto. How are you?" she said when she saw him standing there.

"Fine, thanks, and you? Was it easy to get permission to leave early?"

"Yes, it was. So, where are these houses located?"

"There's a pretty one in Palo Blanco, near the botanical gardens. It's big, and on the inside, it looks a little like the house in El Paraíso," he said excitedly.

"Well. That's nice."

"But would you like to have lunch before we go? Do you have time?" he asked politely.

"I don't mind. I asked for the rest of the day, so I don't have to go back."

"Good. I know a place. The three boys and I go there when they come out with me. They have very good chicken! Would you care to accompany me there?" he suggested.

"Why not?" Gilberto walked on ahead to guide her. She followed, observing that he was sweaty and poorly dressed, but didn't show him that she noticed. On the other hand, she looked splendid, in full bloom at forty, well-dressed, neat, with a slenderness that highlighted her femininity. Her husband now looked like her father rather than her mate; that image was surreal. They quickly arrived at the restaurant and went inside.

"Choose whichever table you like," he said.

"That one in the corner looks fine, doesn't it?"

"Yes, of course."

She smiled naturally. It felt more like a business meeting than a date between a couple. Gilberto was happy, feeling as though he was being granted a miracle. María Sucel, however, wanted to maintain a certain kind of formality between them, to keep a prudent distance from any action that could tangle her up with the past.

"What would you like?" he asked. "There's stew, meat platter; everything is tasty."

"A meat platter. I've been craving one for several days," she replied, trading her seriousness for evident nervousness.

They ate quietly, their eyes on their plates, both stealing looks at each other the whole time. Each shuffled in their mind various conclusions about what would come next, their gazes occasionally crossing nervously.

"Who are the owners of this house?" she asked, breaking the ice.

"He's a nice engineer who owns several houses in the area. He even builds on lots that he buys and then sells the buildings."

"And how did you hear about him?"

"I've been asking various clients to let me know if they hear about a house with a parlor, kitchen, and about five bedrooms. I think it would be good to have my merchandise in the room where I'll sleep. The other rooms are for you and the children. We'll have a pleasant parlor where they can have guests, their friends. Across from the house, there is a park where the neighborhood boys play soccer," he added happily.

Once more, they moved. Their belongings were stowed confidently in a truck whose driver they knew well, for they had moved over twenty times in a decade. Joy over the return to their roots in the northwest preceded this move. Everyone rode in the slatted truck, nestled between mattresses, wardrobes, and kitchen wares. The parents rode in the front with the driver.

After arriving at the house, María Sucel tuned the radio on high volume to the station where her Antonio worked. The music lightened everyone's spirits as they began organizing all the junk in what would be the home of the Cervantes Baroja family in the late '70s.

Here they experienced new joys and felt the spirit of progress. Tomás was accepted into the university, while the others obtained their secondary diplomas in neighborhood schools. It seemed they had finally put to rest their Bogotá restlessness, and in their muted but eager home, each one's hopes were wrapped in enthusiasm.

Outside their home, the city was talking about the death of the millionaire, Rockefeller. The guerrillas had struck another blow by stealing weapons, this time from under the military's own nose. The Andean Pact was moving forward in an effort to disentangle commerce in the region. News stations lauded Pope John Paul II, born Wojtyla, who defended truth and family with words that spoke to the Cervantes' own history. The girls became teens in Palo Blanco, and boys arrived to flirt and hang around the house where three lovely young ladies peeked at them through the windows. It was also in Palo Blanco where, one day, Tomás arrived driving an old jalopy, in which they rode around like rich and famous folks.

However, nothing had changed for Gilberto and for María Sucel. The years witnessed continued distance from each other and their mundane existence. His temples had grayed, and the sun had darkened his skin so much that those who hadn't known him before never imagined he was white. His shoes were increasingly worn out and scuffed, replaced only on Father's Day, courtesy of one or another of his children. And there was no longer any shortage of food, or clothing.

Still Waters

...*1983*

He rested, wrapped up to his neck to ward off the damp chill. His soul couldn't get used to not worrying. At least the traces of pain had eased over the years, and he could forget about them for longer periods. In the small room full of his wares, Gilberto kept company with shadows, his trusted cigarette moving in his mouth like a burning firefly. The one thing that raised his morale was the fact that he occasionally spoke to his wife. However, within those four walls the sound was the same, just whatever was playing on his small radio: a song by Toña la Negra, or a news item announcing that the risk of nuclear devastation had decreased because Carter and Brezhnev were apparently flirting with treaties. Or the news that the Nobel Peace Prize had been awarded to Teresa of Calcutta; or simply that they had freed Hubert Matos from a Cuban prison. None of this even slightly alleviated the gloom in his heart. The nights were long and without affection. Nights that evoked hope and thoughts of the past, first joyful, then turbulent, and nights of disdain.

Peace and prudence reigned in Palo Blanco. Progress came for some, while the older sons' girlfriends occasionally swelled the family ranks. Simply living in a relatively normal way, where the parents were not harassing one another with indifference, had become an achievement that brought a sense of optimism and harmony.

They had been in the Palo Blanco house for eighteen months. Before the sun came up, the cold prompted María Sucel to filter some coffee in an old pot before venturing into the shower to baste her ribs with cold water. Shivering, she dried herself off, rid of yesterday's grime, and came out of the bathroom as the sun rose. Passing by Gilberto's room as she went into the kitchen, she heard a strange moan that stopped her in her tracks. She thought she had heard it coming from his door, but then wondered if it had actually come from the other side of the wall bordering the street. After standing still for a moment, waiting to hear the sound again, she decided that all was quiet and went to have her coffee, before going to her room to get ready to leave for work.

One busy night, María Sucel left work and walked along a downtown street towards the main avenue, where people crowded aboard the public buses, some forced to hang from the doors like bunches of human grapes. This happened every day as one attempted to take public transportation anywhere in the city. Aside from avoiding getting hit by one of the vehicles, her concern was to evade the multitude of pickpockets and purse snatchers waiting to take advantage of people distracted by traffic. They would run off with others' belongings in full view of everyone, without anyone caring. She was mindful of the dangers to which she was exposed on her late commute home. Her only consolation was that she shared this situation with thousands of others who, with humility and self-sacrifice, also worked downtown and offered her their indifferent company.

Arriving at Tenth Avenue, she walked in the direction the buses were coming from, so she could see the signs on their windshields indicating their routes and avoid standing still, thus becoming easy prey for a purse snatcher. María Sucel walked amid the throngs, the colorful buses whisking by only inches from her, weaving in and out of traffic to pick up or drop off passengers. Her eyes watered as she breathed in their exhaust fumes. After walking a block and looking around to make sure she didn't have to worry about the people around her, she stopped and paid attention to the traffic. A woman dressed in rags, holding a little boy by the hand, came up to her, offering lottery tickets for sale with cheerful optimism.

"Friend, buy a lucky ticket for the Bogotá Lottery! I've got a three, I've got an eight! You should buy one, lovely lady, today is your lucky day!" María Sucel shook her head and looked away, taking a step away from the woman, who persisted. "Lady, you'll win for sure! It'll be good to have a few extra pesos!" The woman smiled.

The vendor froze when she felt María Sucel's gaze fixed on her and the little boy. It was as though a bubble had formed around them, isolating them from the noisy traffic, and the woman lowered her gaze sadly. After a tiny instant, she drew her son to her until their bodies were touching, as if shielding him to protect him from María Sucel's compassionate eyes—eyes that unintentionally struck the deepest part of her soul. Something in the boy's movement touched María Sucel deeply. The woman took the boy by the hand and walked away with him quickly, without looking back. Perplexed, María Sucel watched them leave. She followed them with her gaze, taking in every detail, and her hands came up to her cheeks, her face taut with despair. After a few seconds, when she could no longer see the lottery vendor, a small bus already packed full of passengers stopped for her, and she was able to hang on at the door as it pulled away again. The bus left, but her thoughts lingered on the image of that woman and her child's humble face. As best she could, María Sucel made her way inside the vehicle and paid her fare. In the suffocating crush, she felt tears flood her eyes; she couldn't help herself. Some kind passenger took pity on her and got up, courteously offering her a seat; she thanked him with a smile. She felt such sadness, such huge, powerful sadness, among all those commuters.

The ride home lasted less than an hour, enough time to think. Arriving home, she took off her shoes, her earrings, and put away her purse. Piedad was in charge of meals that week and filled a plate for her as soon as she saw her mother. María Sucel saw that most of her children were home and greeted them tiredly. They understood how exhausted she was. Gilberto was in his room that day, as usual. He rarely came out, though there was a roomy parlor with comfortable furniture. Maru and Sara were already at the table, sharing stories about their day.

"I want to tell you about a fragment of life that God showed me today," she told them. "Something so special happened after work today that I haven't been able to rid myself of my fixation on it. I don't know if what I felt was grief or despair." As she went on to relate the details of her encounter, she cried again. The girls surrounded her. Maru wiped the tears from her face, and she continued speaking.

"I was walking on Tenth Avenue after I left work, and a woman with a little boy, about eleven years old, came up to me offering lottery tickets. I ignored her—you know, she looked shabby, and you get fearful of strangers who approach you on Tenth. She sounded like she was from the city, but her face seemed familiar; she looked like she was from the country, like someone from Armenia. I didn't like the look of her and didn't want her to follow me and continue offering lottery tickets, but she insisted. I stepped away to avoid her, but again she insisted, and stood in front of me. The boy with her looked at me with these bright gray eyes, like your father's. When I looked at the lottery vendor, I saw the woman who crushed my hopes and dreams with her stubborn ambition. I saw her there, sunk into the worst human misery, old, her face showing her suffering."

"Who was it, Mama?" Piedad asked.

"Are you sure it was that whore, Ophir? That wretch!" exclaimed Sara angrily.

"Is it true, Mother? Was it her?" wondered Maru.

"It was," she replied. "The one who was battling with me when I didn't even know I was in a war—one that we all lost."

"Why are you crying, Mother?" asked Maru. "You should be laughing madly to see her like that."

"I feel such huge sadness that it feels overwhelming. Imagine, dear. I haven't had a husband accompanying me for over twelve years. I'm saddened by the life we've had to live. Your father is alone in that room dreaming of my company, and as you can see ... that love was paralyzed forever. When a dog struggles to keep two bones, he'll surely never eat a whole bone."

"Does Father know about her?" Sara asked.

"I'll ask him myself," Piedad declared. "I'll do it tomorrow. We almost always talk about how he's doing, or his customers, or his patients. I'll take the opportunity and ask him candidly; surely he'll tell me."

"I'd rather you didn't," said María Sucel. "It might be painful for him to remember that she's alone because of him. Don't ask him anything, please. It's the life we've had to live."

"Have you ever thought about forgiving the old man, and being close to him again?" asked Sara.

"I guess ... I don't know. When I was just a girl, I dreamed of having him my whole life. So many flowers arrived, those flowers that I requested one day in a small acrostic. I was so enamored by them that, for many years, I felt like I was floating on a cotton cloud. But when I realized that the star of my dreams, to whom I'd already given my cluster of babies, was living a parallel life, I dropped off the cloud. Not suddenly, in a second, or a minute, not even in an hour or a day; I have continued falling all these years, and haven't been able to get up because I'm still falling. It's possible that when I finally reach the ground, the hard bump will make me react," she said, biting her lip.

They spoke a long time, the girls asking questions, seeking a way to bring together two alienated souls, and María Sucel reliving her deepest sorrows, justifying her reluctance to attempt any rapprochement.

Night deepened its reign. María Sucel turned off the last light and lay down to think, and to think some more. She thought of Gilberto and for the first time felt sad to think of him alone in his room. She recited The Lord's Prayer, and asked God for a little more strength.

The next day, as she filtered the coffee before her morning bath, she heard again the exact same moan as the day before, and was afraid. She sensed it was Gilberto and decided to check. Silently, she went to the door of his room and placed her right ear against it. Over the sound of the radio, she heard the moan again, but quieter. She was frightened to think he might be in pain and felt sorry for him. Knocking gently on the door, she waited for him to reply, but there was only silence. She knocked again and heard Gilberto's voice from inside the room.

"Who is it?"

"It's me, Maruja. May I come in?"

"Come in," he said. She turned the doorknob and pushed the door open carefully. As she entered, an overwhelming smell of cigarettes overpowered her. She saw him standing by the bed, looking battered, supporting himself with his right hand.

"What is it, Maruja? Is one of the children ill this morning?"

"No, that's not it. I'm here because I've heard moaning lately, and now I've realized that the sounds are coming from this room. Tell me, are you feeling sick? Are you in pain? Those moans are strange."

"I'm fine. Well, I'd say I'm startled from the surprise of this early morning visit. Thank you for your concern. Are you leaving for work already?" he asked her.

"Yes, I'm almost ready. But, are you sure you are all right? I'm worried by what I heard."

"Don't mind the noises I make. I'm old now, and I behave like an old man. At this point, don't all old men invent complaints? Don't worry about a thing, I appreciate it," he said, trying to reassure her.

"Well, if you say so, I'll go, then. By the way, the coffee is hot. Would you like me to bring you a cup?" she asked, still concerned.

"Every morning, at this same time, I smell the coffee as it boils in the pot. Today, it seems that I'll not only smell it, I'll savor it. I'll get up now and pour myself a cup, thank you."

"No, please. I'll bring you a cup. You stay in bed. It's cold."

She went to the kitchen, feeling a certain peace at offering Gilberto some coffee, just like in the old days, when they shared harmony and affection in the hills of Quindío. Wanting to offer him the same thoughtful attention as in the past, she found a matching cup and saucer, and poured the coffee. She added the same amount of sugar as she used to fifteen years earlier, and stirred it. María Sucel took it to his room cheerfully and set the steaming cup on the bedside table. Gilberto watched her and, surprised, smiled contentedly.

"Thank you. Have a good day."

"You too."

Gilberto got up and went to the bathroom, where he rinsed out his mouth and washed as usual. The water was as cold as it was every day. He put a new blade in his razor and shaved carefully. Shivering, a towel wrapped around his waist, he went back to his room and dressed in the same slacks he'd worn the day before and a shirt that one of the girls had ironed and left hanging. He sat on the edge of the bed and pulled his shoes out from under it, then searched for a pair of socks. Needing more light, he pulled open the heavy curtains and threw the handful of socks on the bed, near the light that streamed through the window, and found two matching brown ones. He pulled his socks on and used the ones from the previous day to wipe the dust off his shoes; then he prepared the bundles that he would carry on the black bicycle's grill. A couple of woolen blankets, some tightly packed spreads, and a set of aluminum pots packed in the box from the factory, created a two-foot-tall tower. He went to the picture of Brother José Gregorio Hernández, picked up a crucifix that was sitting on top of his books, and used it to cross himself. He invoked a few saints and left the room, holding the bicycle with both hands. Pushing it along the corridor that bordered the patio, he left the house.

On the street, he moved his left arm in a circle as he rubbed his shoulder with his right hand. He rode down internal streets in the neighborhoods, where there was minimal traffic. In the jacket's right-side pocket, he had his client cards where he kept track of collections, and in his shirt pocket he carried cheap pens in black, blue, and red to make notes about payments and clients. The day's mission was to collect, instead of pushing the heavy cart with metal wheels. Five minutes after starting to pedal, he began to steer the bicycle with his right hand only, at the risk of losing his balance, and while he pedaled, he swung his left arm like a pendulum. He felt internal discomfort, like an intense burning, but chose to think of it as chronic bursitis and blamed a diet too heavy with red meat. At least, that was what the books that he was always reading said, and he accepted that as a wise diagnosis that had never failed the patients that consulted him. The pain got worse as the miles passed, and the arm couldn't hold his weight against the handlebars; he stopped repeatedly, leaning without getting off the bicycle, and again rubbing his shoulder. During one of those pauses, he pulled out a pack of cigarettes from the left pocket of his jacket, lit one and kept it between his lips, meaning to puff on it until it went out. He got back on the road, stopping for five minutes at a time to deal with the discomfort in his shoulder with some spontaneous exercises, then moving on. When the day ended, his pocket was full of cash, his bicycle rack was empty of wares, and strapped to the handlebars were a couple of roses wrapped in newspaper. He tried to protect them from the vibration as the bicycle bumped along the imperfect streets. He arrived home, put away the bicycle and dropped onto his bed, massaging his shoulder again. After a while he got up, unwrapped the pair of roses and carefully broke off each of the threatening thorns and a few leaves that he didn't think looked nice. He took them to the parlor, where other, older roses needed replacing, and, taking the vase to the kitchen, tossed the old roses into the trash. He rinsed and filled the glass vase with fresh water and arranged the new ones and took them to the parlor, where they would remain, like others over the long years, until they withered away. For a few seconds he stood and looked at the roses, then returned to his room. He gathered Kardec's book and the crucifix, and walked to the bed, on which he piled several pillows. Unbuttoning his shirt, he rubbed his shoulder again, placed the crucifix on it and began reading; after a few minutes, the book set aside on the bed, he closed his eyes and pressed the Christ against his shoulder. There he remained, in deep meditation for half an hour, until Maru called him.

"Dad ... Dad ... lunch is ready."

"Thank you, dear. I'll be right there."

Maru withdrew. He buttoned his shirt and walked to the table and sat. He was the only one who hadn't eaten yet, and again, he rubbed his left shoulder with his right hand, trying to ease the discomfort.

"How was your day, Father?" asked Maru as she came into the dining room.

"Fine, dear. Busy. My bicycle rack was empty when I returned."

"You brought some very pretty roses. Who gives them to you?"

"Nobody, dear. I take them from places where nobody cares about them, I've been stealing them with much love for several years. In this land, roses thrive, and then they die, son ... why not take a few to bring beauty to our parlor?"

"You're right, Father. But stealing them? How

embarrassing if they catch you. How do you manage to steal them?"

"I know about forty houses where there are roses in the front yard," he said with a wink. "In a city like this, the only thing people notice growing is concrete and bricks. Most people don't value roses at all. I learned to love them about twenty-five years ago. Back then, every eight days, I used to buy some to give to your mother."

"And are these roses also for her?"

"They will always be for her, but they're also for everyone. It doesn't matter anyway if they're for her," he said sadly. "She no longer appreciates them. Let's say that they're for you, dear, one who thinks they're beautiful. Let's say they're for Piedad, when she smells their aroma. If someday your mother accepts them and appreciates their beauty, then the flowers will be for her."

"Father, we've spoken with Mother at times about the flowers you bring. She told us your beautiful love story, about when she was fifteen and grandfather Elías was unhappy because you were too old for her. We all thought—Mother, too—that you got them from a friend."

"Only God knows, dear, the value I place on these flowers. They will continue to arrive at this house for as long as God gives me strength. It's my meager contribution to this home's happiness. I see that neither your mother nor you girls are aware of my situation. In her case, because she hasn't known about my life during these last years, and you because you've only known my isolation. I'm sorry for you, for me, for her, but it's all right. Life has made me old, and my old age is sullied by resignation. The most important thing is that I love you all very much. By the way, your stew is very good. Thank you, child," he finished.

Days passed, and one day in May, after Mother's

Day, which they had all celebrated in the parlor, a loud wail disturbed the early morning quiet of the house in Palo Blanco. This time, María Sucel panicked. Leaping out of bed and wrapping herself in a blanket, she ran in search of Gilberto. She knew it had been him. As she walked down the hallway, she saw the door to her two older sons' room opening as well, a sliver of light showing. Antonio and Tomás came out with concern while the wailing continued to disturb the serenity of the dawn.

When they entered the room, they found Gilberto sitting on the bed, his shirt off. He was whipping his shoulder with nettles, in a vain attempt to use that pain to eliminate the constant burning sensation eating away at him from inside. It was a bleak thing to see, and his face was even bleaker. María Sucel rushed to his aid, with Antonio and Tomás assisting. Sad and overwhelmed, Gilberto stared at them. He could barely stay sitting. He was panting as he continued to weakly beat the stinging fronds against his back, their burning secretions lacerating his skin. María Sucel took the nettle away and embraced him deeply, fervently. After the beating he had taken, he was so tired. Nothing soothed his pain, and he fell back, overcome by exhaustion.

In a hospital waiting room, the entire Cervantes family sat and waited. María Sucel alone accompanied him for all kinds of tests. After six long hours, she came out, overwhelmed with hopelessness. She told them the doctors had given him painkillers, then sat quietly, her head bowed, bewildered. She rested her head on Sara's shoulder, next to her, and wept inconsolably. Antonio hugged her, and they all imagined the worst.

"What is it, Mother? What does the old man have?"

Tomás asked her.

"Cancer. He has cancer in his lungs, in his stomach, his liver, and even in his left arm. He's dying."

They were a sad group, feeling utterly defeated and powerless, their throats choked by anguish. Gilberto spent a few more hours there, and then they sent him home with specific appointments to begin chemotherapy.

As days went by, his care became more intense. Each member of the family tried to spend as much time as possible with him, time they hadn't taken advantage of before. But the Demerol they had given him kept him in a confused limbo for long hours. Love surfaced, and they struggled intensely to be useful. María Sucel, dejected about his prognosis, dedicated herself to carefully offering him affection. There was little the chemotherapy could do for him now. The cancer had metastasized and was unstoppable.

For five anguished months, the Demerol eased some of his pain, until one long September night, when he was struggling to keep from suffocating, he knew it was time to say goodbye. He no longer had the strength to hide the truth, or to lie. Gilberto was dying, but he had enough awareness to explain some things to his children, things they had never dared ask about. He didn't want to accept blame without first asking for forgiveness. He spoke without prompting, because he needed to, because of his anguish at the idea of dying without a reconciliation. His children had never condemned him, no matter how angry they were, how aware of the situation they were, or how obvious the situation was, or how much they had seen María Sucel suffer and suffer. Only his mother, Sara, when she lived, had tried to straighten him out that faraway day, when, after beating him, she threw him out of the house.

As he spoke, they moistened his lips with vinegar,

as someone had recommended, so he wouldn't die thirsty. Gilberto told them he had never been able to change things at any point in his life; that everything good that had happened to him had been built by María Sucel, and that it weighed on his soul not to have fought for her as she deserved. That he regretted not having valued the things that were most essential, and had settled for letting fate lead him toward bitterness. Until he had seen it in the faces of his loved ones, he had never known suffering; his life had been easy because he had always avoided what was difficult. He told them also that he deeply loved everyone who had suffered because of him. Then, he wished they would learn to live like everyone else, not the way he had lived, because he had never learned to live as he should. He asked them to learn from his mistakes, saying he had never learned, because there had never been punishment for making those mistakes. Raving now, he complained that everyone had always made things easy for him: Nélida pulling him out of the army, Elías keeping his infidelity a secret, María Sucel letting him stay when everything was over, Ophir accepting how far he took things, the coffee pickers .... He told them that life had permitted everything, because it does, but that he had never made correct choices about what he would do.

"I beg your forgiveness," he said, looking desperately at María Sucel, before he died in Tomás' arms.

It was 6:10 in the morning when his soul left his body, with his whole family present. María Sucel knelt and laid her face against his flaccid feet, and kissed them; they all cried as they looked at one another. He was the first member of the Cervantes Baroja family to die. They embraced; the younger ones wept, and the older ones supported them. Tomás lifted his father's defeated body and carried it to a bed that had been prepared for him, spread with neat white sheets; there they laid him down, heartbroken. María Sucel wrapped him in another sheet, tying a white scarf around his head so his mouth wouldn't open. She looked into his gray eyes one last time and closed them forever. The girls brought votive candles, like the ones he had once bought in Armenia to beg the Virgin Mary for María Sucel. Then they left him in the candlelit room until the funeral service that Tomás had hired came for him. In a short while, each of the Cervantes Barojas was wearing black.

Three days later, crowds gathered to bid Brother Gilberto goodbye. The family had never imagined he had been so great. Those who came to honor him shared testimonies of his goodness. All kinds of people came: simple people and haughty ones, adults and young people, women and children tenderly saying farewell. When the coffin was lowered into the ground, María Sucel took a fistful of dirt and tossed it. She took the old worn herbarium from her purse and, opening it, took some dried petals from flowers that he had given her in Armenia and placed them on the coffin, too. From another page, she unfolded a sheet with a poem he had written the day before going to the capital to search for new horizons, and pulling strength from the depths of her soul, she read the first lines:

If I seem distant,
and my face is not peaceful,
don't worry, it's nothing,
I'm just thinking, that's all.

She kissed the poem, and held it against her heart. Supported by the arms of Antonio and Tomás, she watched as the soil covered his presence from this world.

At 6 a.m. on another day, weeks later, the activity at the intercity bus station was exceptionally dynamic and hectic. Some people rushed because the trip depended on them, and others because they were anxious to leave. Sitting in the front passenger seat on a bus, María Sucel sipped a steaming coffee that Acasio Elías had bought her at the station's coffee shop. Juan de Dios sat at her right, thoughtful and serene. Occasionally their eyes met, and she would smile affectionately. The most annoying travelers were the ones who couldn't find enough room for their bags because they had arrived late. Acasio Elías had already placed their suitcases in the bus's upper compartments; the bus had been idling for over half an hour.

Everything was ready for a journey into the past; she thought that going back to the coffee region, if only for a few days, would alleviate their bewilderment at the loss of old Elías and Gilberto. Thinking about not having fully enjoyed Gilberto's presence while he was alive brought them misery. They had undertaken this trip to Armenia in hopes that their hearts might find some consolation in the land where most of the family had been born.

It was a pretty trip because of its significance; the cool breeze coming down from the peaks bordering the highway filtered through the partially open windows of the bus, and the engine's incessant rumbling soon became background noise. People read the day's paper, and everyone talked about the most important thing happening in the country, the kidnapping of the president's brother. According to the newspapers, Fidel Castro had repudiated the notorious kidnapping, although he supported the leftist groups responsible. Other news items reported that one of Colombia's few jumbo jets had crashed near Madrid, and one hundred and seventy-three people had died, including a celebrity or two. Hearing this concerned Acasio Elías, who was unaccustomed to traveling and created tragic scenarios in his mind. But the trip was uneventful, and they stopped only once on the way, for anyone who wanted to go to the bathroom or have something to eat.

Acasio Elías, Juan de Dios, and María Sucel didn't speak much; mostly they looked through the windows at the passing mountain range. María Sucel, however, kept her head against the glass the whole time, at times wiping tears from her cheeks. Juan de Dios knew she was filled with sadness and said nothing. He thought it best that she should cry to rid herself of the despair of her loss. But though he understood, he also felt bitterness touching his young heart. He didn't weep, but his brow was wrinkled as he peered into the deep chasms the bus passed by as it moved on. Acasio Elías mostly remained distant, occasionally saying something that made them laugh.

There were times when they spoke at length, and other long stretches when they were quiet. After passing the mountain range's highest point, called La Línea, in Quindío, the bus began the descent towards Armenia. Their enthusiasm about arriving grew, and their mother's sorrow changed to hope as she thought about once more seeing the places where she had grown up, so full of happiness and harmony. Juan de Dios and Acasio Elías were enraptured by the landscape.

"I think my father took great pride in knowing that Antonio was part of the team broadcasting the *Vuelta a Colombia* bicycle race; they came through here," Acasio Elías commented.

"I saw him crying one day, excited, listening to the radio broadcast of the race, and when he noticed that I was watching him, he wiped his eyes and acted nonchalant. I was embarrassed for him, for he was always the strong, quiet, macho type. And that day I faced him with love and asked him what was wrong. He smiled, somewhat proud and wistful, and told me that he was so happy to hear that my eldest brother was traveling on the highways. When the announcers mentioned his name, Antonio Cervantes Baroja, he was full of pride. Then he was quiet, with his cigarette in his mouth, and I was quiet too. He told me then that sometimes he couldn't help but feel such a deep pride for Antonio and all the rest of us. I told him that I got very excited as well, and that at my school, all my friends knew that he was our brother. The old man was special. I think I love him more than ever now. I don't know why life took him away from me so soon." Juan de Dios pressed his lips together and looked away, to hide his emotion.

"Cesarino told me that some people greeted him at the funeral and said that in a town out on the plains they're building a monument for our father, a little town where he healed and spiritually helped a lot of people. It's incredible that he was so generous," said Acasio Elías.

"What town is it? We could visit it," said Juan de Dios.

"We don't know which town, or who the people are. We should find out. The people who came to the funeral really loved him, and we had him right there with us and barely spoke to him. It's sad, but it's the truth," Acasio Elías said.

"God let you share so much with him," said María Sucel. "It's wonderful. Walking with him next to the cart with metal wheels, visiting clients across the northwest—it was a blessing you carry in your hearts. What was he like with people? Tell me about it. Feed my soul with imagination," she begged, painfully aware that it was her disappointment that had led to her silence and abandonment.

She tried, then, to remember only the happy moments they had shared, so she wouldn't be overwhelmed by sadness. The flowers that never stopped coming, even the Bogotá roses that she had never accepted as hers, paraded across her mind, like the smiles that accompanied their happy moments when each child was born.

"Tell me more," she repeated, looking at Acasio Elías.

"It'll make you sadder."

"It will be a sweet sadness, for it will show me what my husband was like these past fourteen years, Juan de Dios's age. Tell me! Your stories will teach me about things I missed because of how absurd our lives have been."

Acasio Elías looked at Juan de Dios, shrugged, and began to speak.

"All right. One of those many times when he took me with him to work, dragging that heavy iron cart, when we were going through the Santa Rosita neighborhood, a woman came out of a humble house, shouting desperately that her three-year-old son had spilled a pot of boiling water all over his body. Father ran inside, as if pushed by God. He found the boy screaming on the floor, his skin covered with blisters. He put his thumb against his forehead and concentrated, as the woman looked on in amazement. Then, almost immediately, he asked her to bring cooking oil from the kitchen and the other children's school satchels. While the woman went to get those things, people were crowding into the house. She brought the oil, and Father poured it on the boy's body. He dumped the satchel, all the school supplies, on the floor, and he tore the soft plastic cover from one of the notebooks that had fallen out. I remember it was a red plastic cover. Then he asked the boy's mother to cut the covers from the other notebooks while he washed the red one with soap and water. He dried it with a new towel that he was delivering, and began applying the plastic gently on the child's oiled skin. The crowd watched without making a sound, and all we could hear was the child's weeping. His little eyes were looking everywhere, searching for comfort. After a few minutes, the blisters from the burns began to vanish. But the child continued to cry, and Father finished covering his entire body with plastic. Then he placed his finger on his forehead and began to pray with his eyes closed.

"After a few minutes, the child calmed down, and it was very quiet. The people looked at Father like he was a savior. The boy's mother knelt at his feet and then kissed his hand. He told her not to do that and helped her to get up. He said to wait an hour before taking him to a hospital, and said to give him lots of liquids and no fats, so the burns wouldn't get irritated. Finally, he suggested that they not take the plastic off at least until the following day. When we left there, I felt proud to have him as my father. I asked about the plastic. He told me that, this way, the skin would regenerate without scarring. It made sense to me. Then we continued walking."

Moved, María Sucel said, "He was a wonderful man."

The Door Opened

...1994

Under the landing of one of the stairs going up to the second floor, there was a small room that was María Sucel's little fortress, now that she had been promoted to cleaning supervisor. After working for Don Rafael for so many years, he had verbally promised her a small raise, which he hadn't paid her for several months, though she kept reminding him. Nevertheless, she had the responsibility of coordinating the women employees who worked very hard to keep the university clean, much as she herself had in the past. A couple of the women were waiting for her when she arrived, and they greeted her respectfully. María Sucel handed each of them a bucket in which she put supplies and sponges for cleaning. Carrying their buckets, they picked up brooms and mops and went out to battle, without needing further instruction. During the next half hour, more women arrived and likewise went off to their tasks. Then María Sucel prepared coffee with milk; though the university forbade it, with the help of some interested parties she had arranged for the women, one at a time, to have something warm in their stomachs.

One afternoon, when she was checking the various floors of the building, Antonio crept up behind her and surprised her by covering her eyes.

"Who's that?" she asked, intrigued but smiling.

Making his voice sound like an old woman's, Antonio said, "It's old Agnes."

"Who is it?" she asked again, starting to get anxious.

"Take a guess," Antonio said as he uncovered her eyes.

"Son! What are you doing here so early? You should be at the radio station. Did something happen?"

"No, Mother. I asked my boss for the rest of the afternoon off, so I could invite you to lunch at a nice restaurant I know of."

They walked to a fancy Seventh Avenue restaurant, where Antonio requested a table for two.

Flattered, and moved, she said with a smile, "Son, thank you very much for this invitation." She told Antonio that it reminded her of the time Tomás had picked her up in a taxicab to take her to the fundraiser at El Parroquial.

"It's life," replied Antonio. "What is most important is that we're together, and happy. We have great memories of the old man. Remember the time when he worked for months, together with Cesarino, Acasio, and Juan de Dios, to build that house in Rubí, where Tomás wouldn't live, and neither would we?"

"I remember. It was the reason we spoke again after an entire decade."

"Well, the important thing is that he knew that we loved him and appreciated his efforts to provide a home for us. That's when we moved to Palo Blanco, where he died." He signaled to the waiter and asked for a menu and a couple of glasses of wine.

He requested that the strolling singers approach the table. "Have them tune up their guitars and tiples, and prepare their best songs, and I will tip them well afterwards," he exclaimed.

María Sucel looked on in amazement, thinking he was up to something. Giving in to the excitement of the moment, she let the magic surround her. The wine arrived, and the singers began playing lively traditional music, like *bambucos* and *torbellinos*.

Antonio, excited by the atmosphere he had created, offered a toast. "To the one who gave everything she had to make us so happy," he said, standing and kissing her cheek while she gazed at him. "To the old man, who selflessly succumbed to death, leaving behind the pride of being Cervantes," and he raised his glass and his eyes towards the heavens. "In my father's name, I give you the keys to your own home, those keys you once held firmly for several years in El Paraíso, Armenia." Antonio placed a set of keys on the table in front of his mother, who was still trying to make sense of the toast. She raised her glass of wine and, confused, touched it to Antonio's glass. She kept smiling, but consternation wrinkled her brow.

"We'll toast, son. Toast to your father and to all of you. But, please explain what that toast and these keys mean."

"Mother, I've bought you a house, so we can leave Palo Blanco. We can all live together in a house that symbolizes the efforts of the entire family, where we will remember Gilberto Cervantes-Cervantes with joy. It's a new house, in a quiet area of the city, this Bogotá that has seen all our suffering. A place where we can sleep peacefully. The house is yours, Mother. I want you to enjoy it for the rest of your life, and live there with the dignity you had in your house in El Paraíso."

"Promise me that this is true, son! I'm touched by this wonderful news. Do the others know? Who else knows besides me? I never imagined something like this, ever! God bless you, son."

"It doesn't matter who knows. You'll be the first to go inside."

They enjoyed a delicious meal, several wines the establishment recommended, and even had dessert. When they left, they were tipsy with happiness. A cab took them to a place near Palo Blanco. It was a pretty house, with large windows and new paint, inconspicuous considering the large group that would live there. Dignified and charming, it had a large, full-sized kitchen, and hot water in the bathroom to ward off the morning chill and allow a full-body bath every day. María Sucel walked through it a few times, dreaming of how she would decorate it. She stood before a large window and looked out towards the street. She imagined Gilberto walking towards her from a block away, holding a bunch of red flowers and showing them to her as he approached. Lost in her fantasy, she raised her hand to wave to him, but caught herself and glanced quickly at Antonio, discovering that he was watching her.

"What strange thoughts run through your mind, Mother?" he asked, and embraced her lovingly.

"I saw your father walking up from the corner, showing me a bunch of roses as he smiled at me. For a moment I thought that it was real. I miss him so," she said.

"It's life. Nothing lasts forever. But you are very young yet, don't worry," he replied, hugging her close.

"Nor can a body resist," she replied, still holding him.

A week later, the Cervantes family had given their

household things to neighbors, starting with the old battered pots in which they had heated their food over the years, all banged up from so many moves. A new life was beginning for them, and new plans filled their minds. Old Gilberto was no longer with them; that was a truth that they dealt with day after day. As each member of the Cervantes family took on new tasks for the future, they were leaving him behind.

Antonio was going to marry a girl he had met at work. He had a daughter nobody, not even his fiancée, knew about. A girl he had dated years earlier at one of the boarding houses where they had lived had gotten pregnant at sixteen. It seemed that in the mid-'80s, some of Gilberto's sons were following his example, repeating the history of his love affairs, when he would get coffee pickers pregnant in the plantations in Viejo Caldas. Tomás had decided to leave the country. He didn't have any protectors within the company's bureaucracy to help push him forward among the company's chosen ones. He was tired of waiting for a promotion that never came, supposedly because he had graduated from a university other than the University of the Andes. Piedad and Sara were able to finish their schooling, but Maru had not found success. She then produced one of María Sucel's greatest frustrations by getting mixed up in drugs.

This new ordeal consumed her mother's days and nights, and there was little or nothing she could do to fix it. One night, when María Sucel went to find her, in a low-class dump frequented by drug addicts, Maru threatened to stab her if she didn't leave her alone. Plunged once again into a huge problem, the family's frustration grew until finally, in the midst of everyone's despair, Tomás packed a bag with Maru's things and placed it outside the door of the house. By family consensus, aimed at easing María Sucel's suffering and avoiding her emotional collapse, Maru had to leave the house. This marked the triumph of selfishness, but guaranteed peace in the house. Maru left without resistance. She had already decided to leave and was only sleeping at home a few times a week at that point, each time disturbing everyone's rest. María Sucel had developed stomach problems that the doctor attributed to the stress on her nervous system produced by her anguish over Maru.

But before she left, *La Negra*, as they all called Maru, was sarcastic and aggressive, spewing hatred for the family, saying they had never loved her enough. The things she said hit everyone very hard, resonating with each of them, including their terrified mother.

"You are all small, and my world is as large as the earth itself. There's no room for me in this house, because I'm bigger than this space. I've never felt a part of the Cervantes Baroja family. I've never had siblings in my home; you were just acquaintances that I had to prepare meals for, and wash your raggedy clothes. Sometimes I spoke to my father, but we never had a conversation. As for Mother, I just obeyed when she asked me to do something. It's been one disappointment after another, and that just got me accustomed to being unhappy. We were acquaintances who begged for a living, going from one boarding house to another, but every place had the same cold walls and Mother and Father's indifference to each other. I don't care about this pretty house, because in the ugly places where we stayed, nobody knew that I was raped—not just once, several times. Nobody knew that I started smoking dope when I was just a little kid, when the boys were picking through junk. I've been smoking weed for a long time, and the friends I have today, all those Bogotá whores and street people that you're all so scandalized by, they love me. I don't care who we have to steal from or kill in order to live. I don't consider myself a Cervantes, so I don't have to live here. I don't need your pity, because I never had it. Go on struggling to be important in life. I'm not interested in getting on that bus."

Maru picked up her suitcase, turned around, and left. She left, just as Elías had walked away one day in 1966, without looking back. The day María Sucel said goodbye to him when she left Armenia to go to Bogotá forever. That same haunting day when she left Isabelina, looking at her from the other side of the bus window when she moved to Bogotá. Now Maru was doing the same, without looking back, because she had already decided to leave. Bitterly, María Sucel realized that farewells are passed on from parents to children, like an unnatural mutation. The only thing she could do was to pray for her, because no matter what, this was her daughter, whom she loved as only a mother could. She watched her leave and blessed her, asking God to protect her, and hoping that someday she would be back and be a good girl.

Her depression deepened as time went on, lining her face, and the weight of her exhausting life began to show on her forehead. Her brow took on a look of suffering that became permanent, and despair became rooted in her chest, making her feel responsible and guilty about her own unhappiness. A few months later, Tomás left the country with ten years of work experience, a degree under his arm, and a promise to come back for her, to carry her off to brighter horizons. To breathe different air, not tinged with asphalt. This reminded her of Gilberto's promises to her in '66, when he left for Bogotá, supposedly because of the robbery of their home in El Paraíso.

Like dominos, tiles falling one by one, the family broke into fragments and each began their own life. Piedad married a guy called Ignacio, who got her pregnant twice and then abandoned her to my mother's care, who by then was a collector of grandchildren. Of the younger ones, Acasio Elías lived with a co-worker, with whom he had a son; then with another woman, and then another one, as it goes.

One afternoon, the postman blew his whistle outside the house in Bogotá and knocked repeatedly on the door. It was a letter from Tomás, which Sara thought would make their mother happy. The letter told of the difficulties of living in a foreign country, of good challenges and stability in other lands. He said he was thinking of getting married but still hoped to bring her to live with him. He told of working as a dishwasher in a restaurant owned by Jews, and that he had mopped floors in a department store at dawn. Tomás said that, though he needed the work, at least it was honest work, and he didn't feel remorse at no longer working in an office and wearing a tie, as he had in Bogotá, and everyone treating him like he was important. He also said that in the United States, they wouldn't discriminate against her for being a cleaning woman or serving coffee to others. Washing dishes had brought dignity and honor to his life. He also said that even people from good families washed dishes without shame, because, contrary to our own country, in other places washing dishes and cleaning buildings pays well, and brings dignity and happiness. In any case, the dishwashing thing was in the past; now he worked in a small office where he earned enough to be able to send her some money. He promised to also help his brothers and sisters, and said that he would buy her a car when she came to live with him. He would send money so she could get her passport and go to a good doctor for a checkup before leaving.

María Sucel felt hope once again. She would rent out the house that Antonio had bought her, or leave it for Juan de Dios to take care of. Things were in motion; she wanted to leave everything behind and go to her second son, who knew her story so well, the story of her life. She was fifty-two now and had many sons and daughters and grandchildren. But she was still dreadfully lonely, and that loneliness was dragging her towards old age.

Distant family called, and María Sucel took a trip to Manizales. Wearing partial mourning made her look worn, old. She was imbued with an astonishing composure. For eight long hours she rode the bus, moving her fingers, weeping, looking at the vastness of the Andes mountains. The colorful yellow, blue, and red bus in which she rode had soft seats, a television showing Mexican movies, and newspapers with fresh news for the passengers' entertainment. Nothing captured her attention, for this was a sad, fateful trip, to keep an inevitable appointment with destiny. When they arrived at the bus depot in Manizales, María Sucel got off the bus with her canvas bag, looking around uncertainly, unsure of who was coming to pick her up and what they would look like. A couple of women her own age approached curiously, trying to identify any familiar features among the passengers. They also wore partial mourning, with black cashmere shawls to ward off the cold that slithered down from Nevado del Ruiz. María

Sucel recognized them, but then wasn't certain of who they were and whether they would be nice. Generous smiles brought them together.

"Are you Angelina?" asked María Sucel.

"Yes, Aunt, I am ... and this is Estelita. We're so happy to see you. It's too bad that it's because of this sad occasion," she said as they embraced affectionately. It was the first time in decades that they were seeing one another. She had only seen them once or twice in their lives, but they looked like the faded sepia photographs she kept. These were her nieces, the daughters of Bertha and Eliseo, the dynamiter who worked with Elías when he was supervisor. They had come to the station to take her to the house for Isabelina's wake; she had died a few days earlier from old age, with a fractured hip due to osteoporosis.

María Sucel kissed Bertha's cheek when she arrived, then draped herself over her mother's coffin in a heartfelt embrace; she seemed to be asleep for all eternity. Nobody could interrupt the silence. Over the hours that followed, they shared wonderful stories of Isabelina's lovely, fascinating life as they remembered her with gratitude and pride. Bertha told María Sucel that in recent years, Isabelina had stopped praying so much, but she always asked which way Bogotá was, so she could point her blessings in that direction. They also told her she had started begging, and would go to the corner store to ask for coins. According to Bertha, it was just something that old people do. But she said that since everyone in the neighborhood knew her, they would give her coins and ask for her blessing.

"She was a saint," Bertha said.

"She still is, I'd say," added María Sucel. "She was admirable! I remember one day when my father was driving her crazy, asking for his pills for his headache, and she gave him a shirt button to take and the old man's headache was cured."

"God keep her."

It was a simple burial, on a cool day. María Sucel returned to Bogotá, her thoughts filled with concern for others. She recalled previous trips and thought of Gilberto in his youth. Maru, Piedad, and Sara occupied her thoughts especially; she thought they would suffer twice as much in life because they were female. She knew that she had always lived in a macho society, where a woman's hard work was rewarded with indifference and lower pay.

Back in the capital, she realized that she was losing her ties to the past. Elías, Isabelina, Gilberto—they had all journeyed on to infinite remembrance. She thought of them with love and tenderness. While remembering every aspect of her husband's mistakes, his deceit, she felt that the type of life he had led ensured his being forgiven. She avoided reflecting on the misfortunes in her life, which encompassed the whole of it. What remained to her now was her contact with the children she loved with great dedication, whom she understood would only truly appreciate life when they were older, maybe her own age, and there were many years yet before that.

She wasn't returning from burying her mother with a sad heart. More than ever, she understood the insignificance of living, understood that, for a few decades, her only role in this world was to carry in her body the life that had been loaned to her. She would take advantage of the remainder of her life by doing something different, letting circumstances direct her days. Realizing how tired she was of mopping corporate hallways or universities, she felt sorry that she was no longer the cheerful girl from Salamina, Calarcá, or Armenia. María Sucel thought about one day returning to the place she had left, but she knew there was no longer anybody there for her to visit. Her friend Ruby had moved, and she had heard that the house in El Paraíso had become a bus dispatch office. What did it matter? Going back there would only remind her of Ophir.

A few days later, María Sucel left the passport office holding a green booklet with "Colombia" printed across the front, and the hope of showing it at consulates around the world. She knew the passport would be mistrusted at immigration counters in any country she traveled to, but she didn't care, because Tomás had explained that, with dignity, one overcame that. It didn't matter much. Because she was Colombian, she would have the responsibility of proving that she wasn't a bad person, much less a drug trafficker or a guerrilla fighter. She could stand proudly, like any person from France, the U.S., or Great Britain.

"Yes, son, I have my passport. You can send me the ticket now. I'm so happy!" she told Tomás over the phone. "These next two weeks, I'll be seeing the doctor and the dentist. It's best to get that all taken care of before I leave, and not burden you. I love you very much, my dear."

Far from Bogotá, north across the Caribbean, where they don't speak Spanish and dreams of greatness come in barrels, Tomás rested after his day at work. He let the phone ring several times before getting up from his chair. He drank some water. The phone rang again.

"Hello," said Tomás.

"Calling from Bogotá." It was his sister, Sara.

"Hello, Sarita. How are you?"

He listened to her without saying a word, and cold

sweat washed over him. Frustrated, he looked at his wife, who had come in to offer him some coffee. Pulling at his hair, he promised Sarita he would be on the first flight to Bogotá.

The plane left Miami at 4 p.m. and arrived in Bogotá after eight that night. Juan de Dios was waiting for him at the airport, and they took a cab to a clinic in Chapinero, only a few blocks from where María Sucel cleaned every day. They said it was a good clinic because it was where President Betancur had apparently had his appendix removed, and he was fine and had gone on to govern for another couple of years.

As part of the preparations for traveling, a doctor named Ríos had ordered a test for María Sucel with a strange name: an esophagogastroduodenoscopy, or EGD. This doctor inserted a camera down her esophagus in a routine exam, telling her she wasn't to worry, for it was a revolutionary procedure that, like Tarot cards, would show everything inside her. It would only take a few hours, and she was expected home that same afternoon. According to one of Antonio's friends from high school who had become a doctor, the man performing the exam was barely an apprentice, who didn't know what he was doing, and perforated her pancreas.

Tomás barely reached her in time. He hugged her and begged her to get well quickly, so they could leave these places where she had suffered. Then, she could rest, she could meet her daughter-in-law who would soon give her a grandchild, they could walk on the beach by the ocean with their feet bare, and so many other things.

The tubes coming out of her mouth impeded her reply.

The reaction from acute pancreatitis saturated her swollen body. She just opened her eyes with great difficulty, and closed them again.

Silence pervades the funeral home. The door opens, and a flash of light disturbs the eyes of those of us who turn around. It's a delivery man with a crown of tuberoses that someone has sent.

"Flowers for María Sucel!"

END

Also from William Castano-Bedoya

WE THE OTHER PEOPLE: THE BEGGARS OF THE MERCURY LIGHTS
(2023 · English and Spanish Versions Available)

We the Other People -The Beggars of the Mercury Lights- introduces a new voice in American social literature, narrating the relationship between political power and invisible poverty amidst a crisis of conservative values, social injustice, the excesses of extremism, and the politicization of human suffering as a tool of power in the United States.

The story focuses on a family, the Newmans, whose recent economic misfortune has plunged their patriarch into a depressive state in the years leading up to the global health crisis, which forms the backdrop of the novel. Steve Newman struggles to overcome his condition, creating imaginary games in which he blends experiences and fiction as therapy to ward off depression. From his misfortune and desperation emerges the resilience that rescues him from the demons that haunt him, turning him into a more compassionate member of society. Steve must come to terms with his new life, no longer from the height of opulence as he did before his failure, but now knowing firsthand society's abandonment of the poor and the socially 'invisible.' Castaño-Bedoya's novel recreates the lives of those who endure the difficulties of existence under the failure of the Constitution, and who clamor for their universal right to live without fear.

WE'LL MEET IN STOCKHOLM (2024 · English and Spanish Versions Available)

"Being a novelist is less important than living to be one." In the vibrant backdrop of New Orleans' bohemian French Quarter, six independent writers convene at La apassion for writing, they inhabit an old house where they confront the harsh realities of an ever-evolving publishing industry. In this atmosphere of camaraderie and competition, literary aspirations intertwine with the complexities of human relationships.

The novel "We'll meet in Stockholm" pays homage to these courageous writers who strive to be heard in a world often indifferent to their talents. Laden with sarcasm, the title reflects the distant aspiration of winning the coveted Nobel Prize in Literature. For these writers, Stockholm embodies both an ironic utopia and a symbol of La Tertulia's unyielding spirit. Through their intertwined stories, "We'll meet in Stockholm" delves into the complexity of the creative process, friendship, and the sacrifices necessary to pursue a shared passion. It is an exhilarating journey through the heart of creativity, where hope and irony intertwine in the eternal quest for literary greatness.

"LUDOVICO" (2013&2021 · 2023 · English and Spanish Versions Available).

Ludovico. A psychological fictional novel, which recreates Ludovico, a character who narrates in, first-person monologues, his vision of the world despite having, Fragile X mental limitations due to a hereditary condition of mental damage. At first, the reader may think that Ludovico is a character who intends to show us his limited and boring world, but as the story progresses, we discover a primary and elementary orb that does not lack its interpretations, its feelings, its compassion, and its passions. However, the reader faces the great and painful paradox of this novel, which Ludovico suffers and tells unconsciously. The drama of his life, restricted by his poor comprehension, his disobedient vision, and his clumsy ear, condemns him to a fractional understanding that he tries to fill with his fantasy. The story of the one who carries within him an unopened irony and whose simplicity leads us unexpectedly to the borders of laughter and crying. Ludovico lives, like an invisible veil, the double lack of expressing his world and of understanding the one around him.

THE GALPON (2023 · English and Spanish Versions Available)

When the human condition is what directly induces the success or failure of a human being's endeavor, whoever does not evolve goes backwards... Likewise, although supposedly frivolous freedom is currently what governs the global market, its results are ultimately the consequence of man's influence. This is the essence of the corporate world, as William Castaño-Bedoya puts it, in a novel with characters more loyal to profit and fundamentalism than their colleagues and employees. HanssenBox allows itself to wander, led by what its leaders see as destiny, at a time when technology and the online commercial market become industry titans.

Ethan, the company's life manager, and Oliver, an outside consultant, star in that microcosm in a corner of the southeastern United States. The two work under the command of a businessman with a shady disposition who plunges them into episodes of mutual distrust, egocentrism, and insecurity. The lives of the characters are systematically affected by the weight of extremist ideologies and the omnipresence of an underhanded double standard. HanssenBox floats along the passage of circumstances imposed by fate in an era in which e-commerce undertakes a crushing advance without return.

www.ingramcontent.com/pod-product-compliance
Lightning Source LLC
Chambersburg PA
CBHW030255100526
44590CB00012B/406